# DEATH & DYING:

## What You Need to Know—
## Before You Go

## PAM ZARETTA

SandZia Press ● Albuquerque, New Mexico ● USA

Cover design © 2017 by Pam Zaretta
Public domain dancing skeleton artwork courtesy of ClipartPal.com
Special thanks to coverdesignstudio.com

Published by SandZia Press of Albuquerque, New Mexico, U.S.A.

**Library of Congress Control Number: 2017901579**
ISBN-13 (book): 978-1542879675
ISBN-10: 1542879671
First edition/Version 1.0—03/2017
Produced and distributed in the United States of America

# WARNING DISCLAIMER

The purpose of this book is to educate, entertain, and provide accurate information with regard to the subject matter covered. However, the author and publisher accept no responsibility or liability for inaccuracies or omissions. The author and the publisher specifically disclaim any liability, loss, or risk, whether personal, financial or otherwise, that is incurred as a consequence, directly or indirectly, from the use and/or application of any of the contents of this book.

This book is intended to provide information on death and dying, and is sold with the understanding that the publisher and author are not engaged in rendering legal, medical, accounting or other professional services. If legal, medical, financial, or other expert assistance is required, the services of a competent and credentialed professional should be sought.

Every effort has been made to make this book as complete and as accurate as possible. However, there may be mistakes, both typographical and in content. Therefore, this text should be used only as a general guide and not as an ultimate source of information. Further, this book contains information that is current only up to the printing date. The author and publisher shall have neither liability nor responsibility to any person or entity with respect to any loss or damage caused, or alleged to have been caused, directly or indirectly, by the information contained in this book. If you do not wish to be bound by the above, you may return this book to the publisher for a full refund.

# PRODUCT DISCLAIMER

Reference herein to any specific websites, commercial products, process, or service by trade name, trademark, manufacturer, or otherwise, is provided for information, conceptualization and example purposes only, and does not necessarily constitute or imply its endorsement, recommendation, or favoring by the author or publisher.

This book uses material from Wikipedia, under the terms of its Creative Commons Attribution-Share-Alike License 3.0 <http://creativecommons.org/licenses/by-sa/3.0."> and <WP:CC-BY-SA>. Public domain statistics from government agencies are individually cited in the endnotes. Produced with Apache Open Office 4.1.3.

Mistakes, typos, or errata? Contact the author on Twitter @pamzaretta for correction in future editions.

*In loving memory of*

*Dan P. and Tom*

# CONTENTS

# INTRODUCTION

"Every life comes with a death sentence," said Walter White, the fictional, cancer-stricken, high school chemistry teacher-turned-meth-manufacturer in the television series *Breaking Bad*.[1] And it's true—there is not one single recorded instance of immortality in human history. Every person ever born, has died. And that pattern will continue for the foreseeable future, because very old age is the best science and medicine can muster for now.

Several years ago I wrote a generalized (and seemingly innocuous) blog post about death, and why it shouldn't be a taboo subject since it gets us all in the end. It was by far my most popular post, read by more people than all of my other posts combined. At the time, I couldn't figure out why it generated so much interest, particularly for a subject that is not discussed in polite company. And what

I found out from my readers was that many people really do want to know about death, and even talk about it, but they either can't, or don't have an appropriate outlet or platform to do so. My readers wanted to know if people suffer when they die, or is it quick? How does it feel exactly? What happens when families find out a loved one has died? And when we think about our own eventual demise, do we picture it correctly? Are we ever right? Does it end the way we imagined it would, or expect it to?

Death is much easier to face and deal with once you know a little bit about it. It's fascinating and liberating to know what's going to happen and how, because that advance knowledge takes the anxiety and fear of the unknown out of it. This evidence-based book focuses on the scientific and practical aspects of death, from detailed specifics of what physically happens as the body dies (and afterward), to what legally needs to be done both before and after death. It also gives you a good sense statistically of what usually kills people, how it happens, and what it feels like to die from those circumstances—and what you can do to avoid some of them.

Most information about death and dying focuses on the psychological aspects of accepting death, or coping with the loss and grief afterward. But how you *feel* and what you *believe* about death and dying (e.g., Kübler-Ross's work, philosophies of death, etc.) are irrelevant to the pathophysiology of what actually occurs to the body, and what needs to be done legally to ensure your final wishes are carried out as you die—and after you are gone. This book also doesn't address the common themes of emotional and spiritual issues surrounding death because those topics are subjective and different for everyone.

Philosophy, religion, and spirituality are all consolation for the living, and are used to mitigate death, rather than explore or examine the (seemingly) cold facts of it. This book focuses on the physiology, science, and legalities of death that are common to everyone, regardless of beliefs.

At death's doorstep, true power and peace comes from knowing you did what you needed to do, while still healthy and sound, to save your family from a nightmare of expenses, bureaucracy, and complication on top of the grief of your passing. This book gives you the knowledge, confidence, and resources to make that happen.

# CHAPTER ONE

# FACING OBLIVION

No one starts their day expecting to be dead by sunset. And yet each day that's exactly what happens: A woman goes to visit her mother one morning, but never makes it—while en route, she's involved in a fatal car crash. Or a young brain cancer victim finally succumbs to his illness in a hospital one afternoon. Or a teen is killed by a stray bullet from a fight before a concert in the evening.

Aristotle wrote in *Poetics*, "Everything in life has a beginning, a middle, and an end." Even us. Especially us. The strangest part of all is that there is only one way to be born—through the womb—yet there are countless ways to die. And there are many ways life tries to kill us: car accidents, war, terrorism, disease, murders, and natural disasters, to name a few. But all deaths are ultimately the result of permanent brain and heart failure, no matter the cause.

No one knows exactly when or how they will go, even with the best statistics. But statistics do show that less than ten percent of us will die suddenly. The majority of us will die after a long period of illness, with gradual deterioration until the end.[1] In fact, roughly 80 percent of Americans die in a health care facility.[2] Of that number, 63 percent die in hospitals, while 17 percent die in institutional settings such as long-term care facilities.[3] And yet most people don't even really think about their own death until they are well into old age—if they live that long.

Two of the most common reactions to facing one's own eventual death are 1) making a conscious effort to face it or deal with it (few choose this path); or 2) avoidance, absentmindedness, or denial about it (most choose this path). Death is largely an off-limits, taboo topic—bring it up at your next social gathering, and watch how uncomfortable people get, and how quickly they will change the subject. But if people take the time to understand what actually happens, it can remove much of the fear of death and its inevitability.

Television, movies and other media have created a false sense of what the dying process and death are really like. And in real life, death is something vaguely understood from the point of view of family, friends, and medical professionals rather than from genuine, first-hand accounts of what dying actually feels like. That's understandable, because it's just a practical reality that the stages of death don't really allow much room for interviews and documentation as the body shuts down.[4] And medical personnel aren't focused on or trained to talk about it—they are too busy trying to maintain the dying person's comfort.

There are thousands of courses that teach everything from art and accounting to zoning laws. There are an infinite number of birthing classes, but none that teach us how to die, or how to understand death as a normal process, and what to do before, during, and after it happens. Most people have little or no experience with the dying process or death. They haven't watched someone die, nor provided care for someone during the last hours of life. Few people outside of the medical professions have ever seen a dead body. So these things aren't taught, even though everyone will have to face them some day. Information and preparation reduces the fear of death, and understanding the process takes the fear out of the unfamiliar things happening in front of you as you watch a loved one die.

Funeral home director Caleb Wilde states:[5]

> "The North American leap from a culture of healthy death acceptance to a culture of death denial has been no leap at all...And this journey has, in part, been enabled by both the professionalization of death and the funeral industry.
>
> The meta-narrative that we've been given is that death is entirely negative...[which has] made it easier for us to abdicate our responsibilities to the dead and dying over to the 'death and dying professionals,' who have been trained to care for, beautify, and hide the horrors of it.

> But, there's another narrative about
> death...that death can be beautiful...And that
> alternate narrative needs to be discussed.
> Death can allow us to see our own mortality,
> realize our finitude and pursue a meaningful
> life. For the dying, death can be a release of a
> slowly deteriorating body...Contemplating our
> mortality can allow us to pursue vitality. And
> when we embrace death, maybe we can take
> back death care."

Avoidance and denial are totally understandable, of course. Even people who readily argue about politics or money can find themselves suddenly mute when the topic of death is brought up. The bottom line is that most people don't like to think about death, let alone contemplate who is going to get their assets after they die. As a result, people put off estate planning for "someday," which usually turns out to be never. And then the consequences roll in when someone dies: the family can't afford the funeral expenses, or if they can, there isn't enough for other expenses, and it will take awhile to go through probate court to get the deceased's last paycheck and access their bank account. Or the family either can't find the deceased's will, or they don't even know if there is one in the first place. These problems can be eliminated with just a small amount of forethought and action.

Public education about death and dying would increase participation in end-of-life planning (wills, life insurance policies, etc.). The worst time to make plans and decisions is under emotional duress and shock. When a person dies, their family and friends are suddenly tossed into a rough sea of legal and medical decisions they have never faced, and that they are usually completely unfamiliar with. If they haven't prepared for it, it's not easy to navigate through if they don't have a friend or family member who is a lawyer or doctor they can turn to for guidance. The more advance preparation taken, the more time a person's family has to spend saying their goodbyes at the end, instead of trying to make medical and financial decisions through the stress and haze of grief.

So denial and lack of planning won't stop anyone from dying—it will just create a difficult and expensive situation for those left behind. It's easy not to plan ahead, and just hope that everything works out in the end, but that is neither realistic nor fair to loved ones who will have to live with the consequences.  Most people don't want to think about what choices and care they want at the end of life, but if they don't make those decisions, who will do so for them?

Estate planning documents aren't about how much money or how many things you have—they are about you having control over what happens to you as you lay dying, and after you are gone. It's about your wishes being carried out. It's about you deciding who gets what you do have, regardless of the dollar value—and not having a court make those decisions for you. People mistakenly think that wills and other estate planning documents are only for the wealthy, and that lawyers and legal documents are expensive, time-consuming, complicated, and stressful to deal with. They aren't. Once you discover how quick, easy, and inexpensive it is to write a basic will and advanced directive, or create a payable-on-death bank account, you'll wonder why you didn't do it sooner.

# CHAPTER TWO
# CONTROL

Death is proof that we don't have as much control over our life as we like to think we do, because, for the most part, we don't get to choose our time or cause of death, and it happens in spite of our plans. This goes a long way in explaining the fear, denial and avoidance of it.

People leave for work or school in the morning and are dead by sunset due to a car accident, a terror attack, or some other unforeseen incident. People can simply drop dead in the street from a sudden heart attack. Social and behavioral health analyst Julie Framingham observed:[1]

> "Most people in developed countries believe they are in control of their lives and their quality of life...They strongly believe that their actions control their circumstances, as well as events that occur in their lives... It is also assumed that death is something that will happen to an individual only in the future, when one is very old and 'it is their time.'...The illusion of complete control over life events through one's own actions is an

> illusion that is useful when circumstances are favorable, but is shattered by extreme loss and trauma...[such as] a personal crisis or external disaster...Death doesn't happen only to very old people, or those on the nightly news."

The leading killers in the U.S. are heart disease and cancer. Short of genetic predisposition, people actually have a lot of control over lifestyle decisions that can reduce the chances of developing those diseases. In truth, good health is really nothing more than dying at the slowest rate possible.

Where you have lived most of your life, and where you live currently can have a huge influence on your type of death. In some cultures such as Eastern Europe, cigarette smoking is the norm rather than the exception. People in Italy eating a Mediterranean diet are going to have a lot fewer dietary health risks than people in Texas devouring the meat, potatoes and fast foods common to the American diet. Socioeconomic factors also play a role. Citizens of East Liverpool, Ohio, where almost thirty percent of its residents live below the poverty level, reside with one of the world's largest hazardous waste incinerators in their back yards. Wealthy, gated communities in Beverly Park and Laguna Beach, California, would never allow such a thing. Or, you may live in a drug-infested neighborhood with significant gang activity, such as Oklahoma City or Newark, where your likelihood of becoming a victim of violent crime skyrockets compared to living in the middle of nowhere, such as John Day, Oregon.

Environmental factors are important, too, as parts of the communities of Love Canal, New York; Times Beach, Missouri; and the Valley of the Drums in Brooks, Kentucky, are situated on highly-toxic Superfund sites. In fact, the Environmental Protection Agency has found that approximately 17 percent of the U.S. population (53 million people) live within three miles of a Superfund site, including 18 percent of all children under the age of five.[2] Erin Brockovich made Hinckley, California, famous by discovering industrial chromium-6 poisoning in its groundwater supply as the cause of above-average incidence of cancer in its residents.

So what exactly can you control? A lot, actually. Not what strikes in the randomness of life, of course, but you can pro-actively change diet and lifestyle factors, which go a long way toward disease prevention. A study published in the January 2016 medical journal *Nature* found that less than 30 percent of a person's lifetime risk of developing many common types of cancer are due to intrinsic risk factors (i.e., things you can't change, such as genetics).[3] That means you control the other 70 percent. Authors of a September 2016, *Journal of the American Medical Association Oncology* study named four intrinsic lifestyle factors that can change the risk of cancer: obesity, exercise, alcohol consumption, and smoking. The study authors concluded, "A substantial cancer burden may be prevented through lifestyle modification. Primary prevention should remain a priority for cancer control."[4]

Let that sink in for a minute. Cancer doesn't just fall out of sky and attack people randomly.[5] Barring genetic and environmental factors (i.e., you don't live next door to

Chernobyl), you have a very good chance of avoiding cancer by merely addressing four specific things:

**Obesity** – You control what you eat. Educate yourself on what foods are healthy and nutritious, create a program, and implement it.

**Lack of Exercise** – Sedentary lifestyles are killers. The Department of Health and Human Services recommends at least two and a half hours (150 minutes) of moderate aerobic activity, or 75 minutes of vigorous aerobic activity a week, or a combination of both. Aim for at least 30 minutes of physical activity every day. If you can't fit in one 30-minute walk, try three 10-minute walks instead.[6]

**Alcohol** – Most people don't know that alcohol is a mild carcinogen. According to the National Cancer Institute, the more alcohol a person drinks—particularly the more alcohol a person drinks regularly over time—the higher his or her risk of developing an alcohol-associated cancer.[7] One recent study concluded, "There is strong evidence that alcohol causes cancer at seven sites in the body, and probably others. Current estimates suggest that alcohol-attributable cancers at these sites make up 5.8 percent of all cancer deaths world-wide."[8]

In addition to decreasing the likelihood of cancer, lowering alcohol consumption also decreases the risk of fatal accidents that are due to alcohol. So you get twice the control.

**Smoking** – Would you smoke cigarettes if you knew how horrible death from lung cancer is? According to the results of a clinical trial published online by the *Journal of* *the American Medical Association Internal Medicine*, "Affixing pictures on cigarette packs to illustrate the danger of smoking increased attempts by smokers to quit."[9] Unfortunately, you'll have to research those photos that other countries put on their cigarette packs as motivation to quit—sadly a U.S. federal appeals court ruled the proposed warning labels were a violation of Big Tobacco's free speech protections, and banned the use of the images.[10] Luckily, there are plenty of programs that can help people stop smoking, and they aren't as hard to find as those banned images.[11]

So while you can't prevent death itself, you can maybe delay it—perhaps even considerably—and not perish from the diseases generated by those four culprits. If you don't drink, it's highly unlikely you'll die from liver damage (cirrhosis). If you don't smoke, your odds of lung cancer plummet. Diabetes can be avoided, even if genetic, with diet and exercise changes.[12] Find out what other genetic conditions can be mitigated through your own efforts. Making changes won't put a crimp in your quality or enjoyment of life—if anything, it will improve it.

There are other hurdles still to be overcome, though. We con ourselves into believing life is precious and a gift, but the way we live belies it. We poison our environment and threaten our drinking water supplies, harm others for profit through political policies such as deregulation, use drugs and alcohol, eat unhealthy foods, and have sedentary lifestyles, speeding up our demise. We live believing sickness, disease, and disaster will happen to other people, not us. We harm others (including other countries), and then deny it. Would you pollute communities knowing someone's kids and grandkids will suffer the consequences? Would you do it to your own family or community? Would you drink and get behind the wheel of a car knowing it's not just your life at stake, but others' lives as well? If you considered the odds of fatal consequences prior to taking certain actions (as the cigarette warnings proved), it's very likely your perspectives and choices would change.

The reality is people are not taught as a society at large, let alone encouraged, to take the best care of ourselves to live a higher quality of life. Instead, we want to believe that the obese couch potato, or the several-packs-a-day smoker, or the lifelong drunk will all live to be 102, while the kale-eating, 35-year old, vegetarian triathlete will get hit by a bus, or keel over from a stroke, so why bother? We convince ourselves that we'll go when it's "our time" to go, which is far into the future, right? And it will all be over so quickly and painlessly, too. So don't think about it, you have a long ways to go.

Yet you don't, really.

No one wants to live taking 75 pills each morning just to get through the day. There is no harm or downside to taking care of yourself, or planning for the inevitable. Yet sadly, most people cede their control and do neither.

## SUICIDE: THE ULTIMATE CONTROL?

If a person can't control when and how they are born, should they be able to determine when and how they die?

The most direct—and most controversial—way to control one's own death is via suicide, and each year many people do just that. After a period of nearly consistent decline in suicide rates in the U.S. from 1986 through 1999, suicide rates have increased almost steadily from 1999 through 2014, and are now at their highest levels in 30 years.[13] Men take their lives at four times the rate women do, and prefer firearms to do so, whereas women prefer poison.[14]

There are two types of suicide: legal, physician-assisted death, and unsanctioned suicide. They cover two entirely different spectrums of reasons for the act. Physician-assisted death goes by different names in different locales—it is variously called euthanasia, death with dignity, assisted suicide, physician-assisted suicide, and doctor-assisted dying. The names are a bit confusing, because with euthanasia, a doctor has an active role in administering a lethal dose of medication to a patient. In physician-assisted death, the physician only prescribes the fatal drugs, and it is entirely up to the patient to fill the prescription and then take the drugs. But no matter what it's called, the end result is the same.

Physician-assisted death has come a long way since the days of the late Dr. Jack Kevorkian, a Michigan medical pathologist who assisted in patient suicides until his death in 2011. After years of court battles over the legality of his actions, he eventually spent eight years in prison after a 1999 conviction. Kevorkian is credited with sparking a national debate on the ethics of hospice care and "right to die" legislative action.[15] As of 2016, California, Colorado, Oregon, Vermont, and Washington have death with dignity statutes. In December 2008, the

Montana supreme court ruled that physician-assisted suicide is legal after a patient with terminal cancer sued the state. However, Montana still has not established rules and regulations governing the process.[16] Internationally, human euthanasia is legal in the Netherlands, Belgium, Colombia, and Luxembourg. Assisted suicide is legal in Switzerland, Germany, Japan, and Canada.[17]

It's one thing to expect a doctor to do what's best for your health, but what if the patient decides it would be best to avoid prolonged suffering and useless treatment? Dr. Kevorkian once stated, "What difference does it make if someone is terminal? We are all terminal." In his view, a patient did not have to be terminally ill to be assisted in committing suicide, but did need to be suffering. However, he also said that he declined four out of every five assisted suicide requests, on the grounds that the patient needed more treatment, or medical records had to be checked.[18]

The physician-assisted death laws favor the terminally ill and their medical reasons, but the national suicide statistics reflect psychological, biological, and societal factors in addition to health-related reasons. Nationally, the reasons given for unsanctioned suicide deaths are associated statistically with financial concerns, relationship issues, illness, and declining health.[19]

A May 2016 Gallup poll showed that 69 percent of Americans say euthanasia should be legal. (Interestingly, people are more likely to approve of it when the term euthanasia is used, rather than suicide—they may not understand the difference between dying with self-administered drugs, and a doctor actually taking a patients life.) Reasons given for wanting to participate in physician-assisted death programs include concerns over losing autonomy; being less able to engage in activities making life enjoyable; loss of dignity; burdening family, friends, and caregivers; losing control of bodily functions; inadequate pain control or concern about it; and financial implications of treatment.[20] Brooke Jarvis' excellent and beautiful January 2016 *Harper's* magazine essay, "When I Die," illustrates the issue on a personal level by detailing the journey of an Oregon physician with terminal brain cancer through his dying process of assisted suicide.[21]

Understand that physician-assisted death laws in the U.S. don't let just anyone participate—only the terminally ill who have six months or less to live. Cancer is by far the most common reason people choose this method of death.[22] There are strict requirements—you can't just walk in off the street and request a couple bottles of secobarbital. Each state's laws vary, but the basic process is that the applicant has to undergo psychiatric evaluations, and have two or three other physicians review the case and approve it. As such, it's not even close to a same-day service—the duration between the first request that begins the process, and death, can take up to six months, sometimes longer. Some participants go through the process, obtain the medication, and then choose not to use it. Some of them die before they finish the approval process, or receive both approval and the medication, but die before they have a chance to take it. But when they do consume the lethal prescription, the majority of the participants become unconscious within ten minutes, and most die within 90 minutes.[23] The drugs make the patient stop breathing (respiratory arrest).

Like all medical costs these days, physician-assisted death is very expensive, and insurance won't cover the cost of the medication. The two most commonly used drugs are secobarbital (known by the brand name Seconal) in powdered form, and pentobarbital in liquid form (known by the brand name Nembutal).[24] A lethal dose of secobarbital is the most frequently used drug in states with physician-assisted death laws, and costs between $3,000 to $5,000.[25] The inflated price is due to its manufacturer having a monopoly on the drug since there are no generic versions of it available in the U.S.[26] The cost of pentobarbital was roughly $500 until 2012, when the price rose to between $15,000 and $25,000. Manufactured in Denmark as the only liquid form of the drug approved for sale in the U.S., the price increase was caused by the European Union's ban on exports to the U.S. due to pentobarbital being used for lethal injection for capital punishment. Patients then switched to pentobarbital capsules, which cost between $400 and $500, but the powdered form isn't as effective as the liquid, and requires taking almost two full bottles of foul-tasting powder that are usually mixed in juice or applesauce for palatability. To keep such cost fluctuations under control, some states with physician-assisted death laws have created alternate medical formulas that cost between $450 and $600.[27]

Still, such a regimen favors the wealthy. A homeless man who lived in his van in Seattle had lung cancer that spread throughout his body, causing him so much pain that he couldn't walk. Tony Boxwell, a nurse practitioner who treated the man at a local hospital, said, "As he was approaching the end of his life, his desire was to take advantage of the Death With Dignity Act we have here in Washington. The act allows someone to have a place to die and someone with you when you take the $3,000 lethal dose of medicine. And you have to come up with the cash. He's too poor to die. Death was not even an option."[28] But that's not even the most heartbreaking part of his story. "Cancer wasn't the worst thing that happened to [the man in the van]...because somebody broke into his van and shot him in the head, and that's how he died," Boxwell said.[29]

So the issue is complicated by access and cost on top of the legalities. For those who don't seek some form of suicide when facing terminal illness or disease, there are end-of-life care decisions that need to be considered in advance. At what point should medicine shift from trying to cure someone, to a treatment that can provide comfort and control pain? Will the person choose to die at home, or in a hospital? Who will make those kinds of choices if the person is physically or mentally unable to?

And control over health issues is only half the battle. Assets such as money and property—and who they will be passed on to after death—are two more important things people have almost complete control over, but only if they plan ahead. The good news? It's not as complicated or as expensive as most people think, and it doesn't take very long to do at all.

# CHAPTER THREE

# PLANNING AND PREPARING

Advance planning for end-of-life decisions allows a person to retain authority, control, and autonomy over their own death. This is accomplished by preparing legally binding documents well in advance that specify what you want to have happen as you are dying, and after you are dead. If you don't take those steps, then someone else (such as a court, spouse, or physician) will make those decisions for you, and they may not be what you wanted, for religious or other reasons.

In the face of life-threatening illness or other significant change in health status, advance care planning becomes more difficult. People don't make great, informed decisions under duress. As you succumb to illness and the dying process, or during the stress of watching a loved one die, is not the time to start thinking about making end-of-life plans. Planning in advance when your health is stable, and there is no immediacy or urgency, allows your loved ones to focus on spending quality time with you when you're dying. You and your family want to spend the last hours of your life saying your goodbyes, not frantically trying to make plans that could have been done under far less duress while alive.

Creating an estate plan makes it possible for a person to decide in advance who should be in charge of managing their assets, and making decisions for them in case of incapacity or death. (The term "estate" refers to anything you own.) Advance planning allows a person to determine the specific things they want to happen to their financial, health, and legal affairs as they are dying, and after they are gone. The person designates who will take care of their children and other dependents (guardianship), and specifies final gifts or specific bequests to people or organizations, such as charities. They also make decisions about organ donation, autopsy, burial and cremation, funeral planning, and memorial services.

Intestacy laws, wills, trusts, and contractual instruments that bypass probate—such as life insurance policies—are the legal vehicles used to pass property from someone who dies.[1] Without these documents, a person dies "intestate," and their family, friends, and business associates can spend years in court (and often in person) fighting each other over the property.

It costs a lot more to clean up a financial mess after a death, than it does to prevent one by planning ahead. The death of a loved one is an emotional, difficult time for family and friends. The last thing that a person may want to deal with is how to handle the deceased's estate and care for their children (guardianship). Even if you don't particularly care about your own wishes, you should ensure that your survivors aren't handed a tangled, expensive mess after you are gone.

# INTESTATE

The legal term *intestate* means a person died without having a valid will in place. When that happens, their property goes through probate court and is handed down to heirs via state laws known as *intestate succession*. All fifty states have intestacy laws.

Intestate succession distributes the property of the person who died in a way that represents how an average person with a will would have. This default can differ significantly from what the person would have actually wanted. Even where it is known what the person intended, no exceptions are made if no valid will exists. None. Nor are there any exceptions made based on need or special circumstances.[2] The estate will still have to go through probate, and the court gives the deceased's closest surviving relatives everything, including assets and custody over minor children.

People who are not named in a will, such as friends, are generally not recognized by the state as a successor (someone entitled to the deceased's property). In intestate succession, property is handed down through a specific progression of blood relatives (e.g., surviving parents, siblings, grandparents, etc.) until it finally gets turned over to the state itself. Without a will, the decedent's friends, business partners, and other non-relatives who they may have been close to get nothing.

# PROBATE

Probate is a court process by which a will is proved valid or invalid, and the estate of a deceased person is administered.[3] In most states, probate is a three-part, court-supervised process of locating the will and filing an application (petition) for probate; assessing assets and debts and administering the estate after the court approves or validates the will; and closing the will after debts and taxes are paid, and distributing what's left to inheritors and beneficiaries.[4]

Probate is needed to clear titles to land, investments, and bank accounts so that they can be properly transferred and titled into the names of the designated beneficiaries. It's also used to collect debts owed to the deceased, settle disputes as to who is legally entitled to the deceased's assets, and resolve any disputes about the validity of the deceased's will.[5] If a person dies leaving few assets, such as personal belongings or household goods, these items can be distributed among the rightful beneficiaries (such as a spouse and children) without the supervision of the court. But a will would be necessary if you had specific wishes as to who gets what.

Now all of that doesn't sound so terrifying. So why does probate have such a bad rep? The two biggest drawbacks to going through probate are: 1) It can take anywhere from a few months to years, depending on state laws and the complexity of the estate. And an executor can't distribute property, sell assets, or pay off debts until the court grants approval. 2) Probate is expensive. In some states, attorney and court fees can take up to five percent of an estate's value. In addition, there are usually appraiser's fees and other expenses.[6] For example, an estate valued at $100,000 in Missouri would cost $6,600 in executor and attorney's fees.[7] In California, the average cost to probate a $300,000 estate is $9,000. That comes out of your survivor's pockets until the court allows the assets of your estate to be disbursed. Probating an estate without a will is more expensive than probating an estate with a will, and the cost is taken out of the property the heirs would have inherited.[8]

However, probate is not always necessary. Most of a deceased person's property passes to beneficiaries outside of the probate court. Life insurance proceeds and pension money, for example, go directly to the named beneficiary.[9] Probate can also often be avoided without using a living trust by setting up payable-on-death accounts (explained below) and holding assets jointly.[10] If you own bank accounts, vehicles, or property with another person (known as joint ownership), after your death, the surviving co-owner often automatically inherits that property.  If there was no will or joint ownership, the probate court must apply the laws of intestacy for your state.

Another way to bypass probate entirely is under small estate administration proceedings if the decedent's estate is smaller than the dollar amount limits established by state law. (It varies by state, but is generally below $100,000 or $150,000.) When an estate consists of a small home or few valuable assets, then it can qualify as a small estate. A small estate affidavit form is usually accepted to expedite the asset distribution process after someone dies. Your executor completes the form and then files it in the jurisdiction where the property is located.[11] However, some states will not accept the small estate affidavit—see Appendix A to find out what your state's laws are.

## DON'T PROCRASTINATE

Clinicians have observed that the amount of family distress at the time of a death is inversely related to the extent in which advance planning and preparation occurred.[12] Yet many people don't create wills, or do other end-of-life planning because they don't want to make decisions about what will happen to their assets and children after they die. Those choices, however, should be up to you, and not probate courts enforcing state intestacy laws.

Nevertheless, no matter how logical or practical it is, almost two-thirds of Americans over age 35 admit to either not having a will at all, or not having an up-to-date one.[13] (Wealthy people are less likely to have a current will.)[14] A common reason people give for not having a will is that they think they don't have anything to leave. Or, they think it's obvious who will get their property after they die. But without a will or trust in place to specify those wishes, things might not work out at all how they intended, and what they may actually leave behind instead are battles over assets, debts, and mementos.

Some people fear that by planning ahead, they will lose control over their assets. This is untrue, because wills don't take effect until after they die, and living trusts are revocable. Also, most people mistakenly assume their death is far into the future, and that they have many years left before they need to plan for passing along their estate.

The reality is that a tragic fatality can happen anytime, any place.[15]

While the estate planning terminology may be unfamiliar, the process really isn't that difficult. Most people see a bunch of legalese and a mountain of paperwork, with visions of expensive lawyer fees dancing in their heads. So they run the other way, and never get around to it at all. In truth, writing a will (and estate planning in general) is thought to be more difficult than it really is. In some ways, writing a will is far easier than filing your taxes. Overall, estate planning only takes a few days of concentrated effort to complete (think a weekend or two), and then one day a year for maintenance. Most people spend far more time watching TV in a week than it takes to complete an entire estate plan.

A hastily scrawled list on the back of a cocktail napkin or paper bag just won't cut it in court, and oral agreements aren't worth the paper they are printed on. Don't delay creating basic legal documents because of fear of attorneys or their fees. And don't be afraid of making a mistake—you can correct it legally later. It is far better to have a document in place now that you can change or completely revoke later after consulting with an attorney, than to have nothing at all. For example: Let's say Martha has been completely estranged from her biological family for the last 40 years because she totally loathes them. She wants to leave her cars, cash, and salon business to her two best friends. If Martha dies without any estate planning documents (intestate), the laws of her state would most likely give her assets to her estranged family she doesn't want anything to do with. Her two best friends would get nothing.

Now, let's say Martha dies with a will that bequeaths her assets to her two best friends, and absolutely nothing to her biological family. Yes, the estate will still go through probate, and perhaps a revocable living trust would have been better for her financially. But her property still stands an excellent chance of being distributed according to her wishes, even if her biological family contests the will. She's far better off than if she had delayed writing her estate planning documents at all because she wasn't sure if a revocable or irrevocable living trust was best for her, because she never made the time to sit down with an attorney to find out.

It can't be emphasized enough: It's better to have your estate planning wishes legally documented, even if they need to be corrected or amended later, than nothing at all. A few hours of planning ahead will save months or years of expensive heartbreak for your loved ones after you're gone.

## PRINCE: A CASE STUDY IN CONSEQUENCES

Sixty four percent of Americans don't have a will, and many who do don't have an updated one.[16] When it comes to estate planning, you want to leave a legacy behind, rather than an expensive legal and financial nightmare. Here are just a few horror stories of what happens when survivors are left to pick up the pieces when no estate planning was done:[17]

> "My sisters and I have tried to get my father to do something, but he won't. He is almost 90...Dad views any attempt to encourage him as a sign everyone is after his money. He has

no will, no trust, no power of attorney, medical or otherwise. He seems to think that this is his way to control the situation and exert power, and can't see that by doing nothing, he will lose control of how things are handled...I've used myself as an example to try and talk with him. I've told him about my 'death folder,' what all it contains, and my desire to not require my wife and son to have to scramble around not knowing where anything is. I may as well have been talking to the wall."

\* \* \*

"I do occasionally have someone hire me to contest a will, or to contest distribution of an estate without a will. It's always messy, and I usually earn thousands of dollars in the process (which generally comes from the estate). I can think of several situations where a little planning ahead and consultation with an expert could have prevented me from earning large fees."

\* \* \*

"I loved them all [deceased family members], and don't resent having to make arrangements in the aftermaths of their deaths, but it would have been far, far easier if my surviving sister and I didn't have to figure out what to do and how to pay for things within hours of their deaths."

\* \* \*

"A dear unmarried friend had terminal cancer and even after picking out a final resting place, put off drawing up a will...He died

without a will and it was a nightmare for his
family."

* * *

"The deceased won't have to deal with it. It's
the people who are left behind to clean up the
mess who will have all the stress."

* * *

"They would rather you fight over what you
get after they're gone."

Is that the sort of thing you want to leave behind for
your family to deal with? All that sturm and drang over
what is essentially a simple property designation and
distribution list?

Even people who can afford the best lawyers money
can buy don't plan for their deaths, and leave colossal and
expensive legal messes behind that drag on for decades.
That's what happened to many celebrities, including Anna
Nicole Smith, Howard Hughes, and Prince. Some died
without wills, and others had outdated or invalid wills. All
of them involved complicated and prolonged disputes—
and some of the lawsuits have even outlived both the
plaintiff and defendant![18]

The estate of the pop musician Prince is a recent
example that illustrates how expensive, messy, and
bureaucratic things can get when someone dies without a
will. In 2016, Prince (neé Prince Rogers Nelson) died of a
drug overdose at age 57 without a will or named heirs.
The probate process is the same for everyone without a
will, regardless of wealth or status, and the same laws are
applied: Intestate succession laws in Prince's home state

of Minnesota mandated that his estate would pass to his siblings—including his biological sister and his five surviving half-siblings—because his parents are deceased, and he didn't have a spouse or children.[19]

Prince's sister asked the probate court to appoint a special administrator to oversee the settling of the estate. His assets, worth an estimated $300 million, include real property, unreleased music, control of his image, and other intellectual property. Without a will, no one knows for sure what else he may have, or where everything is. He allegedly owns multiple properties in multiple states besides his native Minnesota, and it's unknown how many studio and live albums, music videos, and films he had stored away. Apparently he gave generously to charity, but it's unlikely to continue after his death because he didn't have a will specifying who would benefit, and how much would be donated.[20]

Without a will, anyone can claim certain rights to Prince's property, and the greedy and the weird (such as fake relatives or business partners) always show up when they smell money in high-profile celebrity cases. The probate judge will have to sort through dozens of people who claim to be Prince's blood relatives, those who claim he made oral agreements with them, and his sister and other heirs will have to wait out expert assessments of his physical and intellectual property. Easy probate cases for people who have a will take less than a year to settle if there isn't anything overly complicated. Prince's estate, on the other hand, will take years to sort out, and cost a fortune.[21]

After an expensive contract battle and copyright fight with his record company mid-career, and numerous strained relationships with lawyers, perhaps Prince became gun-shy about being legally bound to *anything* ever again.[22] But had he taken the time to make a will—and honestly, with his fortune, he could more than afford not just one lawyer, but an entire law firm or two—he would have designated a known and trusted executor to manage his property and transfer its assets. Fortunately, the probate judge granted Prince's sister's request to appoint Bremer Trust as special administrator, giving the company authority to manage and supervise Prince's assets, and identify his heirs. The judge approved the ruling because Prince had substantial assets, and owned businesses that required immediate attention and ongoing management.[23] The court-appointed special administrator chose two key figures in Prince's career to manage the entertainment side of his estate: Prince's longtime attorney, manager, and friend L. Londell McMillan; and business executive Charles A. Koppelman.[24]

However, it's very likely there will be family fighting over Prince's estate that could have been avoided with a will or trust. Those documents would have preserved the value of his estate, instead of losing massive amounts of money to fees in fights over it. And once all of that is settled, there's the possibility that the family could sue the parties who helped Prince obtain the opioids that killed him for wrongful death, or sue each other for larger shares of his estate.[25]

So to sum up the mess Prince's death without a will created for his surviving family and the courts to slog through (expensively) for years: No known will, and if one exists, no one knows where it is. No full accounting of assets so no one knows what other property (such as real estate) may exist, or where it is. No one knows who his true heirs are or if there are any "hidden" family members. "Fake" heirs (claimants who have unwritten or oral agreements from Prince, or say they are related to him somehow) have already come forward. Those who are entitled to his estate and property will probably fight over how much of it they can get their hands on. Prince's likeness and royalties will continue to generate income long after his death, so the eventual heirs get to fight over that, too.   The takeaway? Don't think a mess like this applies only to famous, multi-millionaire pop stars or celebrities without a will. Even if you own only a few assets, the same intestacy and probate laws will apply to you if you don't have a legally valid will or trust in place to prevent such a fiasco. There is only one way to prevent trouble, and that's to plan ahead. And if you do, well, you can probably count on a happy ending, like these people did:[26]

> "My husband and I have had wills since we were about 30 or so—maybe younger? And never viewed having a will as worrying about our mortality. It was more a matter of who the heck gets the money when we die!"

> \* \* \*

> "Tomorrow my wife and I go to the closest national cemetery and I turn in the necessary paperwork to 'reserve' our space there— they've already told me they have plenty. Once that's done, we will pre-pay cremation and transport to the cemetery for both of us, and purchase the urns (and not through a funeral

home). Our interment plans will then be a done deal. Next up, have new wills drawn up specifying those arrangements, and dividing whatever estate is left equally between our combined several children. With those plans made (we already have PODs, advance directives, etc.), family won't have a thing they'll have to do or pay for, and nothing to squabble over. We think it is the responsible and caring thing to do."

\* \* \*

"Both my wife's parents and my parents—all long-deceased—had wills and/or revocable trusts established as well as pre-burial arrangements made and paid for. There was no confusion, no additional costs, and we both really appreciated it. That's the example we're following and hope to instill in our children."

\* \* \*

"My grandma, who will turn 90 this year, made her burial arrangements in 1985. She pre-paid...I can't remember how much it cost her, but I know it was less than $2,000. That was very kind of her to think of so many years ago. When my sister passed in 2010, she made sure to show us her papers and give us instructions on what to do when the time came."

Don't do what Prince did. Instead, plan for the inevitable. Your family will thank you, and be grateful to you long after you are gone.

# GETTING STARTED

Estate planning documents are easy to create and maintain. You or your attorney prepare all of the necessary legal documents, sign and notarize them, and then store them all together in a safe place, and tell relevant family members or friends where they're stored. Once a year, review the information to see if any changes or updates need to be made.

If you don't want to do any planning on your own, estate planning lawyers generally offer free initial consultations to see what you need. And many lawyers provide flat-fee estate planning services, creating a will and advanced directives for a fixed sum of a few hundred dollars.

If you want to do most of the work yourself, or if you can't afford a lawyer, there are plenty of self-directed resources online that guide you step-by-step through the creation of each document. (See Appendix A for a list of legal websites offering these services.) Most legal websites use a very intuitive and user-friendly interface to ask you some personal questions, and guide you through the steps to generate wills and other legal documents. The simplicity of the online tools can often be the catalyst to getting the entire job done instead of procrastinating. You can also purchase do-it-yourself will writing software programs instead of using online services.

So whether you hire a lawyer to do everything, or you do it all yourself, the most successful route to estate planning—especially if you have zero familiarity with it— is to break each item into manageable steps by using simple checklists. This can help mitigate the fear of the importance of what you are doing, and build confidence with each successfully completed task. If you don't know how or where to start, there are plenty of checklists online to help walk you through everything step by step. (See Appendix A). Once you get started, momentum builds. Choose one document to work on each week until everything is complete.

Keep in mind that documents created by free or low-cost online legal services are definitely better than not having a will, but they are intended only for simple estates. In more complicated situations involving overseas assets, spouses from other marriages, stepchildren, family businesses, trusts, elaborate investments, or property in multiple states, etc., it's best to consult with a lawyer. You can consult with a local attorney in person, or use an online legal service that has lawyers on staff to answer your specific questions. If you want to work with a local attorney, you can find one through your state bar association, or an online legal referral service (see Appendix A).

Inexpensive as well as free legal advice is widely available online if you can't afford traditional attorney services. Some legal websites charge a low, flat-rate fee, and some allow you to ask limited, general legal questions for free. (See Appendix A for resources.) You can also check with your city or state bar association to see if there are free, non-profit legal clinics you can attend to speak with an attorney. Many law schools also offer free legal clinics.

If you do the work yourself, you can still consult with an attorney if you have any doubts or a complicated situation, or to vet your documents to ensure they are legally binding for your state. Vetting takes less time, and is less expensive than having a lawyer construct all of your documents from start to finish. How good are the online legal tools and services? As a test, I used a low-cost online legal service to generate a will and durable powers of attorney for finance and health. It took less than an hour to do all of it, and I spent less than $50 to use the service. When I had those documents vetted by a traditional attorney charging $300 an hour at a local law firm, the legal documents created by the online service were either identical to or better than (as in more detailed) the documents the lawyer created.

## CHAPTER FOUR
# WHAT YOU NEED FOR WHAT YOU HAVE

This section is to give you a very generalized idea of the legal structures available to you to pass along your property after death. There are a lot of pros and cons and drawbacks that can't possibly all be listed here, so the best thing to do is to decide which one you think would work best for you, and then consult with an attorney.

These are the most commonly used legal structures for estate planning:[1]

| What It Is | What It Does |
|---|---|
| Will | Lets you designate what and how much of your property and assets (estate) you want transferred to the people or organizations you specify (beneficiaries) after your death by appointing someone (executor) to carry out these wishes. Also allows you to appoint someone (guardian) to care for minor children and dependents after your death. |

| What It Is | What It Does |
|---|---|
| Living Trust (revocable and irrevocable) | A living trust is a legal document that, like a will, contains your instructions for what you want to happen to your assets when you die. But—unlike a will—a living trust can avoid probate at death, control all of your assets, and prevent a court from controlling your assets if you become incapacitated.[2] You may need a "pour-over" will to cover minor assets and property that aren't in the trust, and anything not in the trust goes through probate. Also, if you have children, you can't name a guardian for them in a living trust—you'll also need a will.<br><br>Revocable vs. Irrevocable trust: Assets remain in your estate in a revocable trust, but move out of your estate and belong to the trust in an irrevocable trust. This is an important distinction for estate tax purposes since in an irrevocable trust, property is not included in your estate's value for estate tax purposes. Consult with an attorney regarding your specific tax situation to see which trust is best for your situation. |
| **What It Is** | **What It Does** |
| Durable Power of Attorney (for finance and health) | Allows you to designate a person (agent) to make legally binding health or financial decisions for you, and act on your behalf if you become incapacitated and can't make decisions for yourself. |

| What It Is | What It Does |
|------------|--------------|
| Living Will | A living will specifies how you should be cared for in an emergency, or if you are otherwise incapacitated. It sets forth your wishes for resuscitation and other end-of-life treatments, including those you do not want to receive. A living will advises your doctor how to handle your desired treatment. Since you can't account for every contingency, also create a durable power of attorney for health care in addition to a living will.[3] |

So which one is best suited for your current circumstances? If you don't own a lot of assets, or if you have a net worth of less than $50,000, generally a will, payable-on-death accounts, a living will, and durable powers of attorney for finance and health care should cover your needs, even if you have children, are a homeowner, or are a business owner. Check with an attorney to see what works best for your situation. If you have a lot of assets, or a net worth greater than $50,000, consult with an attorney to see if a revocable living trust (or other type of trust not listed here) is preferable over a will for your situation.

Keep in mind that a will or trust isn't something that you create and then forget about until you die. Each year it should be reviewed to see if any changes need to be made. Why? Because if a will is 25 years old and hasn't been updated, it's still a valid will. What exactly needs to be changed or updated? If major changes occur in your life, you might need to update your beneficiaries if you marry or divorce, or if a beneficiary dies before you do, such as a spouse. Other major events, such as the birth of a child, a job loss or promotion, an illness or an inheritance, etc., are always grounds to revisit and revise your planning. Also consider: Have you changed bank accounts? Have any of your beneficiaries moved and changed their phone number or address? Have you acquired new assets (e.g., real estate, boats, cars, etc.) since the previous year? Are there any assets you no longer own that should be removed from the documents? Does your executor and spouse or children know where your documents are? Finally, if you move to another state, the documents will need to be changed to conform to the laws of your new state. So choose a holiday you can remember as a reminder each year, such as Memorial Day, to review your documents and keep them current.

# WILL

A Last Will and Testament ("will" for short) ensures that after you die, your assets are distributed the way you specifically designate them to be. A will doesn't legally take effect until after you've died, and isn't "activated" until it's validated and approved by a probate court.

Basics of a will include your name, address and marital status; the names of your children; the name of who you want as your executor (and backups); and then specific instructions on how you want your property distributed. A will also  appoints a guardian to care for your children, and a guardian to administer finances to support them. You can use a will to bequeath property such as real estate, cash, bank accounts, stocks, bonds, intellectual property (such as royalties, copyrights, patents, etc.), and furniture, cars, artwork, collections, jewelry, etc. Most states require witness signatures and notarization of your will for it to be valid.

The remaining assets you don't specifically bequeath to specific people (beneficiaries) are considered the *residuary estate*. This includes non-sentimental or non-valuable items such as knick-knacks, photo albums, kitchen items, tools or furniture, etc. A person known as a *residuary beneficiary* should be designated in your will to take this leftover property and disperse it as they see fit, such as donating it to charity, or selling it online and donating the proceeds. So if your brother insists on owning your plastic pink flamingo lawn ornaments, and you didn't specifically give them to him in your will, he has to slug it out with the residual beneficiary to get them.

Many people write a will hoping that it will last a lifetime, but changes in family situations like marriage, divorce, births and deaths can all render a will obsolete at best, and actually quite troublesome if not updated.[4] You can amend or change your will anytime by drafting and executing a codicil (amendment) to the will, or creating an entirely new will, because some attorneys won't draft a codicil to a will that was written by another attorney. You can revoke your entire will at any time before you die, and replace it with a new one that states all previous wills are no longer valid. You can also specifically disinherit people.

Wills are public documents, so don't put confidential or secure information such as computer passwords or Social Security numbers in them.

There are many free estate planning checklists available to make sure you have everything you need to get started (See Appendix A for resources). Wills are quick and inexpensive to create, and you can make things easy for yourself (or your lawyer) by drawing up a list of all assets and property you own, and naming who you'd like to receive what (beneficiaries). Then, the lawyer can take care of the technicalities required by your state's laws. Keep this "rough draft" simple by focusing exactly on what you want to have happen. The basic formula to do this is:

> *Upon my death, I want my money (how much) and the things I own (name the specific items) to be given to the following people (name them individually) and/or organizations (name them specifically) in the following amounts (how much).*

For example: "Upon my death I want $10,000 cash and 20 gold coins and 30 silver coins, as well as my entire vinyl record collection, to be given to my co-worker David Brown." Or, "I want my purple leather sofa to be given to my sister Sue Smith," or "Please donate my 2010 Maserati GranTurismo to the Boston Humane Society."

You'll definitely need help from an attorney if your assets are scattered across different states, or if you want to give your assets to multiple people (such as splitting a business you own into thirds to give to each of your three children in equal shares). Generally, the more complicated the assets and ownership, and the more beneficiaries you name, the more you should consult with a lawyer to make sure everything is legally sound.

Next, think about who you want to appoint as your executor to make all of this happen. This person files your will with the probate court, pays bills and taxes for your estate, and distributes your assets to the people you specified (beneficiaries) in your will. Make sure you have another person (or two) designated as alternate executors in case your first choice precedes you in death, can't serve for some other reason (e.g., incapacitated, on active duty overseas in the military, etc.), or refuses to.

If you have minor children or dependent adults, select who you'd like to be their guardian, and who you would like to have manage their finances (guardian of their estate) since some state laws don't allow children to own more than a small amount of property (roughly $5,000 or less). This doesn't have to be the same person; some people are good with kids and some people are good with money, but not both. Make sure you have a couple of people in reserve as alternate guardians, too.

If you have pets, you'll need to ensure they are taken care of after you die. There are three documents you can use to accomplish this. One is to include the instructions in your will. Another is a free-standing, traditional pet trust. This trust enlists a trustee who distributes funds and ensures that the person caring for your pets follows your instructions. Finally, a pet protection agreement (PPA) is a layperson's pet trust—an affordable, fill-in-the-blank, legally enforceable document.[5]

In your will, appoint a digital executor who will access your computer, email, social media accounts, and other online services. Many people own media on iTunes, have documents in cloud storage, and have digital family photos stored online that shouldn't be inaccessible or lost forever. The digital executor can access and retrieve these items, and close all of your online accounts.

Trusts, contracts, and co-ownership of property supersede directives in a will. For example, if your life insurance policy requires a designated beneficiary, then the proceeds would bypass probate and go directly to your named beneficiary regardless of intestacy laws.

Although it's not against the law to include your burial plans in a will, it may be futile. One reason is that settling the estate and probate proceedings usually don't happen until after the funeral. So if your only funeral instructions are found in the will, then your loved ones may not be aware of your funeral wishes until after it's too late.[6] Lawyers recommend creating a separate document, known as a "Final Arrangements" document (see Appendix A). You can use this document to address a wide range of issues, such as whether you want burial, cremation, or embalming; your choice of casket or container; how your remains will be transported to the facility of your choice; ceremony arrangements for your funeral and/or burial; your wishes for who your pallbearers will be; and your choice of tombstone or cemetery marker. If you don't specify these things in writing, and you have not clearly communicated your wishes to your loved ones, state law may fill the void by assigning a surviving relative—usually a spouse or children—to make funeral and burial decisions.[7]

# REVOCABLE AND IRREVOCABLE TRUSTS

Living trusts allow people to legally avoid probate. The term "living" means that the trust goes into effect during the life of the person creating it (grantor). Revocable means the trust can be changed at any time after it is created, while an irrevocable trust is a type of trust that can't be changed after the agreement has been signed.[8]

The most common trusts are revocable living trusts. This means you have the right and the ability to nullify the trust itself and either create a new one, or use other estate planning documents to organize your affairs. An irrevocable trust, on the other hand, is more complicated, and is generally used for people with a lot of assets. There are many different kinds of irrevocable trusts, and they are designed for estate tax reduction, asset protection, and charitable estate planning.

The advantage of holding property in a trust is that after your death, the trust property is not part of your probate estate. (It is, however, counted as part of your estate for federal estate tax purposes.) Most trust owners appoint themselves as trustee, and enjoy the property in the trust while alive. The trust owns the assets within it, even though you may still have full use of them. In a trust document, you specify who you want to inherit the trust property, just like a will.[9] After your death, a successor trustee can easily and quickly transfer the trust property to the family or friends you leave it to. By skipping probate, trust assets are generally distributed much faster to heirs—usually within weeks, rather than the months or years it can take with a will. Your successor trustee will pay your debts and distribute your assets according to your instructions.[10] Trusts are also harder to contest than wills.

Trusts are recommended if you own assets in another state (it saves heirs from probate in that state); worry that in case of disability you will be unduly influenced; wish to create other types of trusts within your living trust that don't require court oversight; some of your beneficiaries are disabled; or you live in a state with burdensome and costly probate processes. Simply writing up a living trust doesn't fund the trust. You have to "fund" the trust by transferring each of your assets—such as bank accounts, property titles, etc.—into the trust through separate paperwork. A trust can only cover assets that are placed in it; otherwise a probate court has to sort through what is left out of it.

Typical assets funding a trust include real estate, stocks, CDs, bank accounts, investments, insurance, and assets with titles. Most living trusts also include jewelry, clothes, art, furniture, and other assets that don't have titles. Some beneficiary designations (i.e., insurance policies) can also be changed to a trust so a court can't control them if a beneficiary is incapacitated or no longer living when you die. (IRAs, 401(k)s, etc., can be exceptions, so check with an attorney.)[11]

Drafting a living trust usually costs more than drafting a will, since it's a more complex legal document. While a living trust makes sense for some people, wills are just fine for others. For people with simple estates or few assets, such as young, married couples without kids, a living trust is probably not financially advantageous. A general rule among tax planners is that the larger the value of the estate, the greater need there is for a living trust. If you have a lot of assets, or a net worth greater than $50,000, consult with an attorney to see which kind of trust is right for you.

# LIVING TRUST OR WILL?

Laws vary from state to state, but there are several differences between a will and a living trust. The most important difference is that living trusts avoid probate, which saves court expenses and gets your assets to your heirs quicker. Another important difference involves the transfer of property. With a will, you simply specify the property and who you want it to go to, and in what amount. On the other hand, trusts must be funded by transferring the property separately into the trust. You can still use the property in the trust while you're alive, but you won't technically be the owner—the trust is.

In almost all states, you can't name a guardian for your children with a living trust—you must use a will, and the guardian must be approved by the court. Parents of small children often make both a will and a living trust.

When pop superstar Michael Jackson died at age 50 of an accidental drug overdose, he left behind three minor children. Jackson had both a will and a revocable living trust. Because Jackson's estate was a trust-based estate and not a will-based estate, his will was really nothing more than a pour-over will. So Jackson's revocable living trust controlled who would inherit what, and when.[12]

Unlike wills, living trusts are private, and assets are shielded from the public. Under normal circumstances, Jackson's trust agreement would be a private document that only family members and those named in the trust could read. But because of Michael Jackson's fame, a redacted copy of the Michael Jackson Family Trust was generously released to the public by his attorney a year after the singer's death.[13]

Wills become public documents once they are filed in probate court, and it's very rare that a judge will seal the will after it's filed. Why is that important, since you'll be dead and won't care if anyone can see your entire probate file? One big reason is that the file will reveal what you owned, who you owed money to, and who stands to inherit your estate. Anyone can read the obituary page, go down to the court, and request and read the probate filings, which include each heir's name and address as well as those of the executor. You couldn't send a more golden invitation to potential thieves or con men. Also, disinherited heirs and bill collectors can read the documents and possibly contest the will, or sue the estate.[14]

## OTHER VITAL DOCUMENTS

Wills and living trusts are only one piece of an estate plan. Other documents that are equally important include: a) health care directives such as a living will and/or durable power of attorney for health care; b) a durable power of attorney for finances; and c) a disposition authorization and letter of final arrangements (burial wishes).

Don't let the idea of needing several documents discourage you into inaction. It isn't overwhelming at all, and most of it is very straightforward. Once you have your core information such as beneficiaries and executors figured out, the information in each document is repetitive (name, address, etc.) so they don't take long to complete. Some of them, such as payable- and transfer-on-death accounts (explained below) take less than ten minutes to complete.

There are checklists in Appendix A that explain what you need for each document, where to find forms for free, and how to complete them. Pick one document at a time to work on for a couple of hours a week until it's complete, and then move on to the next one. You'll find each piece gets easier as you go along. Once everything is completed, signed and notarized (check your particular state's requirements, or ask an attorney), the documents are legally binding, but can be revoked or amended by you at any time.

# ADVANCE DIRECTIVES

Documents such as a health care power of attorney and a living will provide guidelines for medical decision making if you are incapacitated and can't make those decisions yourself. The need for such documents has been highlighted by several court cases that received national attention (such as Terri Schiavo, discussed below), where family members and doctors disagreed on the point at which life-preserving machines should be disconnected, necessitating a court's involvement.[15]

To some, it's obvious at what point they want the plug pulled, but they need specific legal documents outlining their choices for others to comply with when the time comes. Health care directives are the legal documents that allow you to specify your end-of-life medical care ahead of time. If you become incapacitated and unable to communicate, these documents inform medical personnel and caregivers of medical treatment you do and don't want given to you. For example: If you were in a car accident on the way home from a night out with your friends, and you fell into a coma for several weeks, who would make medical decisions on your behalf? Who would be able to access your checking account to pay your mortgage and other bills? The consequences of a catastrophic accident by not planning ahead for one are very real.

There are two types of health care directives: a durable power of attorney for health care, and living wills. The "durable" in a durable power of attorney means that your instructions remain valid even if you become incapacitated or are unable to make decisions for yourself. If a power of attorney document does not explicitly say that the power is durable, it ends if you become incapacitated.[16] A health care durable power of attorney authorizes a person whom you select (also called a proxy, agent, or surrogate) to make health care decisions if you are unable to. This person generally has power to provide medical decisions that aren't covered in your living will; can hire and fire doctors and caregivers providing your treatment; enforce your healthcare wishes in court; access your medical records and has visitation rights.[17] By having durable power of attorney documents, you can avoid a court-appointed conservator for your affairs. Your agent acts as your advocate if there are issues with your living will, or disagreements within your family about your preferred healthcare strategy.[18] Since someone else has the power to decide your medical treatment, be careful when choosing this option, and be sure to pick someone who knows what you want, and who is willing to carry out those wishes for you on your behalf. Contact an attorney if you want language inserted in the documents that limits the power to specific decisions. Durable power of attorney documents can be canceled or revoked at any time via a written notice to your agent. (For free "Notice of Revocation" forms online for your state, see Appendix A).

A living will (also called a *directive to physicians* or *advanced directive*) is a legal document that specifies the medical treatments you do or don't want at the end of life if you are unable to communicate your wishes. It includes whether you accept or refuse artificial life support such as a feeding tube or respirator. The intent is to prevent dilemmas that could arise if you are afflicted with an incurable or irreversible condition that will inevitably lead to death. It also prevents medical treatments that would prolong the dying process. The key thing to remember with a living will is that you are specifying what *you* want ahead of time and not giving that power to anyone else.[19] It leaves the decisions in your hands in advance, for when you won't be able to make them yourself later.

So with a living will, you designate your specific medical wishes, while with a durable power of attorney for healthcare, a person you designate (your agent) makes those health care decisions for you. There are pros and cons to each, so be sure to check with an attorney to see what is best for your specific situation. These documents ensure your wishes will be respected and carried out, even if your family members or caregivers don't agree with them.

One famous case that illustrates the utmost importance of health care directives is that of Terri Schiavo. At the age of 26, Schiavo suffered a cardiac arrest in her St. Petersburg, Florida, home on February 25, 1990. She was resuscitated, but had massive brain damage due to lack of oxygen to her brain, and was left comatose. After two and a half months without improvement, her diagnosis was changed to that of a persistent vegetative state requiring prolonged artificial life support. There were numerous court battles for years over whether or not life support for her should be discontinued. Schiavo's husband insisted that she had voiced her desire never to live under such conditions, while her parents fought to keep her sustained by artificial means. Eventually, the court sided with her husband, and she died in 2005 after life support was discontinued.[20] (An autopsy on Schiavo backed her husband's contention that she was in a persistent vegetative state, finding that she had massive and irreversible brain damage.)[21] Had Schiavo executed an advanced directive, her family would have definitively known her wishes, rather than fighting about what she may have wanted for 15 years.

Another directive known as a durable power of attorney for finance is highly recommended in addition to the healthcare documents. The durable power of attorney for finance lets you designate someone to act on your behalf (a legal surrogate) to handle financial affairs and transactions for you. This includes bank deposits and withdrawals, real estate transactions, mail pickup, car loan payments, and tax payments. Some financial institutions won't honor a durable power of attorney for finance unless it is documented on their own forms, so check with your financial companies to see what they require. Contact an attorney if you are concerned that you may be giving someone too much power to control your money so that the attorney can insert language that limits or restricts usage.[22] (Durable powers of attorney are less risky when used with living trusts, rather than alone.)

A do-not-resuscitate (DNR) order is a physician's written order instructing healthcare providers (such as paramedics or hospital personnel) not to attempt CPR in case of cardiac or respiratory arrest. Unlike a living will or a medical power of attorney, a person cannot prepare a DNR order; it must be prepared and signed by a physician to be valid. A DNR order should also be included with a living will, and you can also ask your doctor to add a DNR order to your medical records.[23]

If things become very dire, you can also have your physician complete a Physician Order for Life-Sustaining Treatment (POLST) form. POLST is not an advance directive, but an actionable medical order intended only for seriously ill patients not expected to live for more than a year. The POLST form is a medical order for specific medical treatments you want during a medical emergency. Only individuals with a serious illness or advanced frailty near the end of life need a POLST form.[24]

After you sign and notarize these documents, make two copies. Give the original document to your agent, give one copy to your alternate agent, and keep the second copy for yourself. At the designated time you are unable to make decisions for yourself, your agent will take the documents to your medical providers, bank, school, and other places to make decisions and sign contracts as if they were you.[25]

# PODs & TODs

Payable-on-death (POD) accounts have been called the "poor man's trust" perhaps because they give you total control of the assets within the accounts (no matter how large the amount) during your lifetime, and avoid probate upon your death. PODs are used for bank accounts, certificates of deposit, and some types of retirement accounts (many don't require PODs so check with your financial adviser or the custodian of the account to be sure).

To convert your already existing accounts to PODs, simply request the free forms from your financial institution, designate the beneficiaries whom you want to inherit the money in the account(s) after you die, sign and notarize the forms, and then return them to the financial institution (keep copies for yourself, obviously). The beneficiaries you specify won't have any rights to the money until after you die, so you can spend it all or change who you want to leave it to at any time. After your death, the beneficiary presents the financial institution with your death certificate and their identification, and the money goes directly to them, completely bypassing probate.[26]

Transfer-on-death (TOD) accounts work in a similar manner as PODs, but are mostly used for stocks and bonds and brokerage accounts. Again, request the free TOD forms from the company, complete, sign and notarize the forms, and return them to the brokerage. The beneficiary you name in the TOD form will inherit the account automatically upon your death, avoiding probate just like POD accounts. The beneficiary works directly with the brokerage company to transfer the account after your death.

Some states give vehicle owners the option of naming a beneficiary on the vehicle's registration form in order to bequeath a vehicle to someone without going through probate. It's a simple, free, and effective way to pass on cars, trucks, and small boats. You can change your mind at any time, but a downside is you can't name an alternate beneficiary. States that currently have transfer-on-death registration are: Arizona, Arkansas, California, Connecticut, Delaware, Illinois, Indiana, Kansas, Missouri, Nebraska, Nevada, Ohio, Vermont, and Virginia. Check with your local Department of Motor Vehicles to find out how to register.[27]

Rather than go through the expense and hassle of creating and maintaining a living trust to transfer real estate without probate, in some states you can set up a TOD deed, also known as a beneficiary deed. It's very similar to using a POD for a bank account, because you name beneficiaries and they inherit the property after you die without going through probate. (However, if there's debt or a mortgage affiliated with the land, your death doesn't erase it.) Once you've signed the TOD deed, file it with the local government's auditor or recorder's office where the property is located, or it won't be valid.

The TOD deed beneficiary will have to do the paperwork (usually requiring an affidavit and a copy of the death certificate) to transfer the property into their name. You can change your mind (or your beneficiaries) at any time. If your state law doesn't allow TOD deeds, you can't use one, and will need a will or living trust to transfer the property. If your real estate or title company doesn't have forms for TOD deeds, you will need a lawyer to write a TOD deed that adheres to the specific laws of the state the property is in. (This is a rare time I don't recommend using online legal forms to do this.) At the time of this writing, the following 26 states (plus Washington, D.C.) allow TOD deeds, even if you are not a resident of that state (check with an attorney to see if your state has been added since).[28]

| | | | |
|---|---|---|---|
| Alaska | Hawaii | Nebraska | South Dakota |
| Arizona | Illinois | Nevada | Texas |
| Arkansas | Indiana | New Mexico | Virginia |
| California | Kansas | North Dakota | Washington |
| Colorado | Minnesota | Ohio | West Virginia |
| District of | Missouri | Oklahoma | Wisconsin |
| Columbia | Montana | Oregon | Wyoming |

# LIFE INSURANCE

Life insurance policies are a financial product intended to provide financial support to your dependents if you die prematurely. Though the rules that apply to life insurance payouts vary from state to state, in general, upon your death, life insurance policies pay a lump sum of cash (known as a death benefit) to your stated beneficiary and avoids probate. It will pay the costs of a funeral and other expenses, including debts, loans, estate taxes, non-major medical bills, and family living expenses for awhile. You can also designate in your will how you specifically want the life insurance funds to be used. The IRS states that, "Generally, life insurance proceeds you receive as a beneficiary due to the death of the insured person aren't includable in gross income and you don't have report them. However, any interest you receive is taxable and you should report it as interest received."[29]

A basic life insurance policy for non-smokers under 40 years old costs roughly between $400-$500 per year.

If you want a traditional funeral, but don't have life insurance or some other readily available financial means to cover funeral expenses, your options dwindle considerably.

# FUNERAL EXPENSES

There are an average of 2.4 million funerals per year in the U.S., and it's an estimated $20.7 billion a year industry.[30] When it comes to your actual funeral, keep in mind that you don't need to go for broke, literally. Funerals are for the living, and you are going to eventually end up as worm food no matter whether your casket cost $500 or $500,000. So be practical and realistic, and remember that how much friends and family love you is not measured by how much they spend on your final farewell party. One problem is that thanks to movies and television, many people who never saved for their funeral and don't have life insurance still expect a full service extravaganza, not realizing that flowers, caskets, burial, limousines, hearses, and obituaries all cost money—and lots of it. The average funeral in the U.S. costs between $8,000 to $10,000.[31] If you don't finance your funeral with a life insurance policy or other funds, then the costs get paid out of your estate—if there's enough money and property of value left to cover the bill.

Planning ahead for your funeral ensures that you have control over where and how you're buried or cremated, what services or ceremonies you prefer, and the budget for it all. Just before or immediately after someone's death is not the time to plan or budget for a funeral, because people rarely make good decisions under duress, and your survivors can only guess what you might have wanted. For those who have never made funeral arrangements, planning can be an additional stress because of the short window of time for final disposition of the body. Also, choosing a funeral home that's nearby, or one family or friends used before, or purchasing an expensive funeral package without comparing prices just to get the whole thing over with, are not necessarily good choices.[32] Families often have the deceased's remains sent to a funeral home with no real idea of the full cost, not realizing that most funeral homes must be paid up front (because it's hard to repo a dead body).

The great boxing champion, Muhammad Ali, spent *years* planning for his funeral—a three-day farewell. "We're here to do the job the way I want it," he said during the planning. Ali used a large notebook to outline the details (the book containing it was two inches thick), planning all of the events that took place in his hometown of Louisville, Kentucky. This included a long, slow procession through the city streets, an arena-sized memorial service, and an Islamic-based funeral with multiple religious participants.[33] (If you don't know how or where to start with funeral planning, see Appendix A for resources that walk you through it step-by-step.)

Since a will is not usually read until after the funeral, it's not a good place to indicate your funeral preferences. A disposition authorization is a notarized legal document that allows you to authorize your choice of cremation or burial, and designate where you'd like your final resting place to be. (See Appendix A for examples.) Complete the form, sign and notarize it, and keep it with your other important estate planning papers. Compose a final arrangements letter to your family that outlines specific details for your funeral itself (such as who you want as pallbearers, what type of music you want played, etc.) and file it with the disposition authorization. Be sure to discuss your wishes in advance with your loved ones, and let them know where the documents are filed so they can present them to the funeral home after your death.[34]

Funeral home prices can vary by thousands of dollars, so shop around for a funeral provider long before you need one, as it's really no different than planning for a wedding or other expensive event. Some funeral homes even list their prices online. Be vigilant, because the field has been ripe for abuse and price-gouging over the years. The Funeral Consumers Alliance has free resources on how to plan and not get ripped off (see Appendix A). For example, embalming is expensive and only required under certain conditions. According to the Funeral Information Society:

> "Embalming is rarely required by law. The Federal Trade Commission and many state regulators require that funeral directors inform consumers that embalming is not required except in certain special cases. Embalming is required when crossing state lines from Alabama, Alaska, and New Jersey. Three other states—Idaho, Kansas, and Minnesota—require embalming when a body is shipped by common carrier."
>
> – From the pamphlet *What You Should Know About Embalming*[35]

Prepaid funeral plans are an option, but a risky one and not recommended. One reason is that people are living longer, and many funeral homes have gone out of business in the last twenty years. If that happens to you, there's little chance you'll ever see your money returned to you. Also, promises made by the representative who signed the contract with you aren't always agreed upon or honored after you're gone. Since the funeral home holds your corpse, they have more leverage over your grieving relatives in an argument. Also, according to Josh Slocum, executive director of the Funeral Consumers Alliance: "Some prepaid plans can actually cost you more in payments over time than the amount they'll pay out for your funeral." Finally, if you move or relocate after purchasing the prepaid plan, those funds cannot be transferred to another funeral home because the original plan is specific to the one you signed the prepaid agreement with. So let the money stay in your savings account and in your control (and eventually, your POD beneficiary's control). This is why setting your bank account up for a POD transfer of funds (provided you have enough cash in it, of course) is a better option, because at least it will earn interest, be available for an emergency, and still provide financial support when you pass away.[36]

One way to save money on funeral expenses is to purchase items like the casket, urn, or grave marker from other, third-party merchants instead of a funeral home. You can purchase caskets online from well-known discount and warehouse retailers (i.e., Costco) for roughly $1,500. For cremations, you can buy sets of small urns so family members in different cities can each take home some of a loved one's cremated remains. There are numerous companies selling funeral products online, and these can cost a fraction of funeral home prices. And federal law requires all funeral homes to accept funeral products bought from third parties, and they cannot charge you extra for doing so.[37]

With more than half of Americans living paycheck to paycheck, and roughly 15 percent of Americans below the poverty line, many families don't have the funds or other means to pay for a funeral—especially when the death is sudden and unexpected. If you have to make funeral arrangements with no life insurance or burial insurance policy to help cover the costs, and you have little means to pay for a funeral, then you'll need some low-cost options.[38]

In 2016, the nationwide cremation rate was about 50 percent, up from 25 percent in 1999.[39] Unlike burial, direct cremation (also called immediate cremation or basic cremation) is the least expensive final disposition method. In a direct cremation, a simple cardboard cremation container is used, the cremation is conducted with no viewing, services, or ceremony, and the cremated remains are returned to the family within a week in a temporary container, unless a cremation urn is selected in advance. Prices in the U.S. for direct cremation range from $500 to $2,000, depending on your city. Urns can be buried or ashes scattered, and there can be a formal funeral either before or after a person is cremated even though there's no casket to bury. Since funeral homes are in the business of maximizing profits, you may have to contact several funeral homes to find one that offers direct cremation, since many don't publicize it.

Nonprofit organizations may be able to help cover the funeral costs of someone who dies without life insurance, savings, or affluent family members. The government might also be able to help. Below are a few organizations you can try to find funeral financial assistance, but you may not be able to obtain enough to cover the entire cost.

**Social Security Death Benefits:** The Social Security survivors benefits program pays a special, one-time, lump sum amount of $255 to help pay for funeral or burial costs for anyone who qualified for Social Security benefits.[40] This one-off payment is made to a surviving spouse or child. Contact Social Security (see Appendix A), or a funeral director can often help you make a claim with them.

**Veteran's Benefits:** The Veterans Administration will pay up to $749 toward burial and funeral expenses for deaths on or after October 1, 2016 (if hospitalized by VA at the time of death), or $300 toward burial and funeral expenses (if not hospitalized by VA at the time of death), and a $749 plot interment allowance (if not buried in a national cemetery).[41] The armed forces and veterans affairs also have several charities that help with funeral expenses for people who qualify for economic hardship.

**Crime Victims' Compensation Program:** Each state has a Crime Victims' Compensation Program fund set up to financially assist victims of crime, and the fund helps cover funeral expenses. Contact your state's Crime Victims' Compensation Program to find out if help is available.

**Government grants for funeral expenses:** If your loved one died during a natural disaster, or due to negligence on the part of an organization, you might qualify for a special government grant. The Federal Emergency Management Association (FEMA) provides individual grants and family grants during natural disasters. For non-disasters, you can contact your local social services or public health department to see if they have funding to help, or if they can refer you to other local resources.

Sometimes you can obtain assistance from organizations that the deceased or family is a member of, such as churches, unions, and trade or fraternal organizations. Alternatively, certain charities in your area may be able to help cover some of the costs associated with your loved one's burial. Most religious charities offer such support for members of specific denominations. It's likely that you'll have to contact several different charities and secure funding from multiple sources.[42]

Nonprofit mortuaries are rare, but they do exist in some areas; search online to see if there is one near you.[43] Finally, if all other options have been exhausted to no avail, survivors can set up a crowdfunding page online to cover funeral expenses. The deceased's friends, family, and social media circles may want to contribute as a way to say goodbye.

Very poor and low-income survivors are usually in for horrible sticker shock on top of their grief. When poor people die, their options are very limited, just like in life. Because death is such a major expense, for those who absolutely cannot afford a funeral of any kind, there are really only two options available: 1) donating the body to medical science, or 2) leaving it unclaimed, or to be disposed of within an "indigent remains" program run by your local government.

There are whole-body donation medical programs throughout the U.S. that use cadavers for surgical education and training. While it may seem unnerving to some, donating the body to medical science is actually a very reasonable solution. The receiving scientific institution typically handles all of the costs. The body is used for instruction and research by the medical profession, and then cremated. The ashes are then returned at no cost to the family. The whole process takes between four to six weeks, and a memorial service can take place afterward, if desired. Note that medical donation often requires the prior consent of the deceased, so you absolutely have to plan ahead. (See Appendix A for companies that offer whole-body donation.)

Indigent remains programs provide cremation and proper burial for individuals who are penniless or destitute, and serves people whose families either could not be located or could not provide for the proper disposition of remains. Typically in these programs, the indigent decedents are cremated and then stored in a secure location at a coroner's or medical examiner's office until a ceremony and burial are held every year or two. The decedents are buried in individual containers in shared plots, and records are kept for each one so that they may be recovered at a later point in time if a family member requests.[44]

So research the funeral homes in your area to get an idea of funeral costs, and come up with a couple of solutions on how to finance it when your time comes. Make sure to document those plans in your final arrangements letter or disposition authorization.

## PUTTING IT ALL TOGETHER

The last thing you want to do is send your grieving family scurrying around looking for wills, contracts, policies, statements, and other documents that will be needed to settle your affairs. It is better to keep all of your important documents in one file for family members so they will have everything handy, and won't have to scramble around in a desperate search for documents during a difficult and stressful time. (See Appendix C for information on creating a master document file.) Keep everything organized together, and then let the people who will need it upon your death know where it is. You can make a large binder or file to store the documents in, and then let your spouse, executor or trustee, and attorney know where it's located. Make sure your doctors have copies of your advance directives. Don't store your documents in a safe deposit box, because other people will need access to them before (for health care directives) and after your death (will).

Think about it: If it takes you an hour or two (or longer) for you to get all of your documents organized, imagine how long it would take a grieving relative who not only has no idea where to look for them, but doesn't even know if they exist or not. If you need help organizing, books such as Cullen and Irving's *Get It Together: Organize Your Records So Your Family Won't Have To,* and planning kits such as *Before I Go, You Should Know* from the Funeral Consumers Alliance, can help you keep track of what you need and how to store it.[45]

Estate planning isn't a massive time investment once you're committed to it, even if you do most of the work yourself instead of hiring an attorney. It ultimately boils down to just two steps: Create, sign, and notarize the legally binding documents, and then gather all the information in one master file and tell the people you trust most (spouse, executor, etc.) where all of it is stored.

Below is a basic estate planning to-do list. See Appendices A and B for checklists and free resources to create these documents.

- Create a will or trust. If creating a trust, make sure to fund the trust with your assets.

- Create an advance directive for both health and finances, and a living will.

- Ask your doctor to create a do-not-resuscitate order (DNR) if you want one.

- Complete a disposition authorization to state your specific wishes for funeral arrangements, burial or cremation, and organ donation. Write a final arrangements letter detailing how you want the funeral ceremony conducted.

- Give copies of the healthcare documents to your doctor, attorney, and family members or friends.

- Compile all the original documents together into one master file, and tell your spouse, attorney and other family members its location.

How simple and easy is some of this? Here's an example for setting up your bank accounts to be payable-on-death (POD) accounts:

Step 1—Request the forms (they are free) from the bank (or other financial institution) by phone, email or snail mail. Total time: five minutes. Total cost: nothing.

Step 2—Fill out POD forms upon receipt. Total time: ten minutes, max. Total cost: nothing.

Step 3—Have the POD forms witnessed and notarized at the bank (free if you have an account). Total time: fifteen minutes. Total cost: nothing.

So setting up POD accounts just took 30 minutes (probably less), and cost absolutely nothing. Now your beneficiaries can have instant access to the money to pay expenses after you die, instead of having it tied up in probate for months or years.

Thirty minutes max. Free. You know you have the time—you spend more time on social media and watching television. Get started now. You know you can do it.

# CHAPTER FIVE

# WHEN (& HOW) YOU'LL MOST LIKELY GO

In general, there are four basic ways to die. Some people will perish in accidents (cars, falling), violently (war or crime), willingly (suicide), or naturally (disease). The average life expectancy in the U.S. is 78.8 years—that's 76.4 years for males and 81.2 years for females.[1] So most Americans won't die instantly, or even quickly, but will instead experience a more drawn-out, lingering illness or degenerative disease before succumbing.

Once again, wealth and poverty play a major factor in how you go: People in high-income countries live longer than people in poor countries. In wealthy, first-world countries, most deaths (seven out of ten) are among people age 70 or older, and they die mostly from chronic diseases: cardiovascular diseases, cancers, dementia, chronic obstructive lung disease, or diabetes.[2] In poorer, third-world countries, four in ten deaths are children under 15 years old, while only two out of ten deaths are among people aged 70 or older. People in poorer nations predominantly succumb to infectious diseases such as lower respiratory infections, HIV/AIDS, diarrheal diseases, malaria, and tuberculosis, which collectively account for almost one third of all deaths.[3]

In the U.S., the Centers for Disease Control (CDC) in Atlanta; and internationally, the World Health Organization (WHO) in Switzerland, compile data and statistics that give a pretty good idea of what will eventually kill us. Here are the top five:

| Top Five Leading Causes of Death in the U.S and the World – Comparison | |
|---|---|
| **United States (2015 data)[4]** | **World (2012 data)[5]** |
| 1) Heart disease: 614,348 people | 1) Heart disease – 7.4 million people |
| 2) Cancer: 591,699 people | 2) Stroke – 6.7 million people |
| 3) Chronic lower respiratory diseases/CLRD (bronchitis and emphysema):[6] 147,101 people | 3) Chronic Obstructive Lung Disease/COPD[7] (e.g. Bronchitis, emphysema) – 3.1 million people |
| 4) Accidents (unintentional injuries): 136,053 people | 4) Lower respiratory infections (e.g. pneumonia) – 3.1 million people |
| 5) Stroke (cerebrovascular diseases): 133,103 people | 5) Trachea, bronchus and lung cancers – 1.6 million people |

In the U.S., the top five causes listed above accounted for 63 percent of all deaths.[8] Again, relating it all back to how much control you have over how you are going to die mentioned earlier, the CDC estimates that 15 percent of these cancer deaths, 30 percent of these heart-disease deaths, 43 percent of these unintentional-injury deaths, 36 percent of these respiratory deaths, and 28 percent of these stroke deaths were potentially preventable (defined as "premature deaths that could have been avoided.")[9] This is accomplished through prevention efforts by health care providers, who can advise and counsel patients on prevention programs to help them quit smoking, prevent heart disease and stroke with diet modification and exercise, and avoid unintentional injuries.[10]

The following chart, based on CDC data, shows the general leading causes of death by age group in the U.S.[11] (The most recent data is for 2014 and sometimes 2015; it lags behind because it takes a couple years to receive and compile data from the states, who have to compile it from the counties, etc.). In other words, this shows how the majority of people your age die:[12]

(SEE NEXT PAGE)

**<u>Chart 1</u> © 2017 Centers for Disease Control.
Used with permission.**
(https://www.cdc.gov/injury/wisqars/leadingcauses.html)
Data Source:
National Vital Statistics System,
National Center for Health Statistics, CDC.
Produced By: National Center for Injury Prevention &
Control, CDC using WISQARS

(Note: White squares represent deaths from diseases and health conditions; colored squares represent injury-based deaths.)

## 10 Leading Causes of Death by Age Group, United States – 2014

| Rank | <1 | 1-4 | 5-9 | 10-14 | 15-24 | 25-34 | 35-44 | 45-54 | 55-64 | 65+ | Total |
|---|---|---|---|---|---|---|---|---|---|---|---|
| 1 | Congenital Anomalies 4,746 | Unintentional Injury 1,216 | Unintentional Injury 730 | Unintentional Injury 750 | Unintentional Injury 11,836 | Unintentional Injury 17,357 | Unintentional Injury 16,048 | Malignant Neoplasms 44,834 | Malignant Neoplasms 115,282 | Heart Disease 489,722 | Heart Disease 614,348 |
| 2 | Short Gestation 4,173 | Congenital Anomalies 399 | Malignant Neoplasms 436 | Suicide 425 | Suicide 5,079 | Suicide 6,569 | Malignant Neoplasms 11,267 | Heart Disease 34,791 | Heart Disease 74,473 | Malignant Neoplasms 413,885 | Malignant Neoplasms 591,699 |
| 3 | Maternal Pregnancy Comp. 1,574 | Homicide 364 | Congenital Anomalies 192 | Malignant Neoplasms 416 | Homicide 4,144 | Homicide 4,159 | Heart Disease 10,368 | Unintentional Injury 20,610 | Unintentional Injury 18,030 | Chronic Low. Respiratory Disease 124,693 | Chronic Low. Respiratory Disease 147,101 |
| 4 | SIDS 1,545 | Malignant Neoplasms 321 | Homicide 123 | Congenital Anomalies 156 | Malignant Neoplasms 1,569 | Malignant Neoplasms 3,624 | Suicide 6,706 | Suicide 8,767 | Chronic Low. Respiratory Disease 16,492 | Cerebro-vascular 113,308 | Unintentional Injury 136,053 |
| 5 | Unintentional Injury 1,161 | Heart Disease 149 | Heart Disease 69 | Homicide 156 | Heart Disease 953 | Heart Disease 3,341 | Homicide 2,588 | Liver Disease 8,627 | Diabetes Mellitus 13,342 | Alzheimer's Disease 92,604 | Cerebro-vascular 133,103 |
| 6 | Placenta Cord. Membranes 965 | Influenza & Pneumonia 109 | Chronic Low. Respiratory Disease 68 | Heart Disease 122 | Congenital Anomalies 377 | Liver Disease 725 | Liver Disease 2,582 | Diabetes Mellitus 6,062 | Liver Disease 12,792 | Diabetes Mellitus 54,161 | Alzheimer's Disease 93,541 |
| 7 | Bacterial Sepsis 544 | Chronic Low Respiratory Disease 53 | Influenza & Pneumonia 57 | Chronic Low Respiratory Disease 71 | Influenza & Pneumonia 199 | Diabetes Mellitus 709 | Diabetes Mellitus 1,999 | Cerebro-vascular 5,349 | Cerebro-vascular 11,727 | Unintentional Injury 48,295 | Diabetes Mellitus 76,488 |
| 8 | Respiratory Distress 460 | Septicemia 53 | Cerebro-vascular 45 | Cerebro-vascular 43 | Diabetes Mellitus 181 | HIV 583 | Cerebro-vascular 1,745 | Chronic Low. Respiratory Disease 4,402 | Suicide 7,527 | Influenza & Pneumonia 44,836 | Influenza & Pneumonia 55,227 |
| 9 | Circulatory System Disease 444 | Benign Neoplasms 38 | Benign Neoplasms 36 | Influenza & Pneumonia 41 | Chronic Low Respiratory Disease 178 | Cerebro-vascular 579 | HIV 1,174 | Influenza & Pneumonia 2,731 | Septicemia 5,709 | Nephritis 39,957 | Nephritis 48,146 |
| 10 | Neonatal Hemorrhage 441 | Perinatal Period 38 | Septicemia 33 | Benign Neoplasms 38 | Cerebro-vascular 177 | Influenza & Pneumonia 549 | Influenza & Pneumonia 1,125 | Septicemia 2,514 | Influenza & Pneumonia 5,390 | Septicemia 29,124 | Suicide 42,773 |

So basically, people between a year old and age 44 die from unintentional injuries (described below). Should they survive that, from age 45 to 64, malignant neoplasms (cancer) will most likely get them. And should they survive injury and cancer, from the age of 65 onward, heart disease is lurking for them.

While most of the categories are self-explanatory, what exactly does "unintentional injury" mean? The next chart explains it in detail.

(SEE NEXT PAGE)

**<u>Chart 2</u> © 2017 Centers for Disease Control.
Used with permission.**
(https://www.cdc.gov/injury/wisqars/leadingcauses.html)

Data Source:
National Vital Statistics System,
National Center for Health Statistics, CDC.
Produced By: National Center for Injury Prevention &
Control, CDC using WISQARS

(Note: The colored squares highlight specific "unintentional" causes of death, while the white squares represent violent causes of death.)

## 10 Leading Causes of Injury Deaths by Age Group Highlighting Unintentional Injury Deaths, United States – 2014

| Rank | <1 | 1-4 | 5-9 | 10-14 | 15-24 | 25-34 | 35-44 | 45-54 | 55-64 | 65+ | Total |
|---|---|---|---|---|---|---|---|---|---|---|---|
| 1 | Unintentional Suffocation 991 | Unintentional Drowning 388 | Unintentional MV Traffic 345 | Unintentional MV Traffic 384 | Unintentional MV Traffic 6,531 | Unintentional Poisoning 9,334 | Unintentional Poisoning 9,116 | Unintentional Poisoning 11,009 | Unintentional Poisoning 7,013 | Unintentional Fall 27,044 | Unintentional Poisoning 42,032 |
| 2 | Homicide Unspecified 119 | Unintentional MV Traffic 293 | Unintentional Drowning 125 | Suicide Suffocation 225 | Homicide Firearm 3,587 | Unintentional MV Traffic 5,856 | Unintentional MV Traffic 4,308 | Unintentional MV Traffic 5,024 | Unintentional MV Traffic 4,554 | Unintentional MV Traffic 6,373 | Unintentional MV Traffic 33,736 |
| 3 | Homicide Other Spec., Classifiable 83 | Homicide Unspecified 149 | Unintentional Fire/Burn 68 | Suicide Firearm 174 | Unintentional Poisoning 3,482 | Homicide Firearm 3,260 | Suicide Firearm 2,830 | Suicide Firearm 3,953 | Suicide Firearm 3,910 | Suicide Firearm 5,367 | Unintentional Fall 31,959 |
| 4 | Unintentional MV Traffic 61 | Unintentional Suffocation 120 | Homicide Firearm 58 | Homicide Firearm 115 | Suicide Firearm 2,270 | Suicide Firearm 2,829 | Suicide Suffocation 2,057 | Suicide Suffocation 2,321 | Unintentional Fall 2,558 | Unintentional Unspecified 4,590 | Suicide Firearm 21,334 |
| 5 | Undetermined Suffocation 40 | Unintentional Fire/Burn 117 | Unintentional Other Land Transport 36 | Unintentional Drowning 105 | Suicide Suffocation 2,010 | Suicide Suffocation 2,402 | Homicide Firearm 1,835 | Suicide Poisoning 1,795 | Suicide Poisoning 1,529 | Unintentional Suffocation 3,692 | Suicide Suffocation 11,407 |
| 6 | Unintentional Drowning 29 | Unintentional Pedestrian, Other 107 | Unintentional Suffocation 34 | Unintentional Fire/Burn 49 | Unintentional Drowning 507 | Suicide Poisoning 800 | Suicide Poisoning 1,274 | Unintentional Fall 1,340 | Unintentional Suffocation 1,509 | Unintentional Poisoning 1,993 | Homicide Firearm 10,945 |
| 7 | Homicide Suffocation 26 | Homicide Other Spec., Classifiable 73 | Unintentional Natural/ Environment 22 | Unintentional Other Land Transport 49 | Suicide Poisoning 363 | Undetermined Poisoning 575 | Undetermined Poisoning 637 | Homicide Firearm 1,132 | Undetermined Poisoning 698 | Adverse Effects 1,554 | Suicide Poisoning 6,808 |
| 8 | Unintentional Natural/ Environment 17 | Homicide Firearm 47 | Unintentional Pedestrian, Other 18 | Unintentional Suffocation 33 | Homicide Cut/Pierce 314 | Homicide Cut/Pierce 430 | Unintentional Fall 504 | Undetermined Poisoning 820 | Undetermined Poisoning 539 | Unintentional Fire/Burn 1,151 | Unintentional Suffocation 6,580 |
| 9 | Undetermined Unspecified 16 | Unintentional Struck by or Against 38 | Unintentional Struck by or Against 16 | Unintentional Poisoning 22 | Undetermined Poisoning 229 | Unintentional Drowning 399 | Unintentional Drowning 363 | Unintentional Suffocation 452 | Homicide Firearm 538 | Suicide Poisoning 1,028 | Unintentional Unspecified 5,848 |
| 10 | Unintentional Fire/Burn 15 | Unintentional Natural/ Environment 35 | Unintentional Firearm (Tied) 14 | Homicide Cut/Pierce 19 | Unintentional Other Land Transport 177 | Unintentional Fall 285 | Homicide Cut/Pierce 313 | Unintentional Drowning 442 | Unintentional Unspecified 530 | Suicide Suffocation 880 | Unintentional Drowning 3,406 |

Again, most of the categories are self-explanatory, but a couple can be clarified. In the case of 10- to 24-year olds, unintentional injury deaths are due to unintentional motor vehicle traffic, which is a scientific way of saying car or motorcycle accident. From ages 25 to 64, the unintentional injury is specifically unintentional poisoning, which is defined as a person taking too much of a substance, but didn't mean to cause harm.[13] That's the scientific way of saying "accidental drug overdose," which refers to both legal (prescription and over-the-counter) and illegal (street drugs like heroin and cocaine) substances.[14] The person intended to take the drug, but not harm themselves doing it. If they *did* intend to harm themselves with the drug, the overdose is classified as a suicide.[15] (Unintentional poisoning does not usually include deaths due only to alcohol.)

So drug overdoses are the leading cause of unintentional injury in the U.S. because the country is in the middle of an opioid epidemic, which is preventable to a large extent by mandating physicians to stop writing so many inappropriate prescriptions for them.[16] Fentanyl, which killed the pop musician Prince, was created to ease the pain of cancer patients and others who might sustain agony in death. It was never meant to be used to manage pain in daily life.[17] But thanks to political lobbying and lack of oversight, opioids became profit machines for their Big Pharma manufacturers, creating a horrific human toll.[18] According to Joseph Rannazzisi, former head of the Drug Enforcement Agency (DEA) office responsible for preventing prescription medicine abuse, "Drug companies and their lobbyists have a 'stranglehold' on Congress to protect a $9 billion-a-year trade in opioid painkillers, claiming the lives of nearly 19,000 people a year."[19] According to the CDC, since 1999, the amount of prescription opioids sold in the U.S. nearly quadrupled, yet there has not been an overall change in the amount of pain that Americans report.[20] "Fewer Americans are dying young from preventable causes of death," says former CDC Director Tom Frieden. "Tragically, deaths from overdose are increasing because of the opioid epidemic, and there are still large differences between states in all preventable causes of death, indicating that many more lives can be saved through use of prevention and treatment available today."[21]

So the first two charts highlight general, unintentional deaths, focusing mostly on illness and accidents. The third chart of CDC data  highlights deliberate injury deaths, which are due to violence.

**Chart 3** © **2017 Centers for Disease Control.**
**Used with permission.**
(https://www.cdc.gov/injury/wisqars/leadingcauses.html)
Data Source:
National Vital Statistics System,
National Center for Health Statistics, CDC.
Produced By: National Center for Injury Prevention &
Control, CDC using WISQARS

(Note: The colored squares highlight intentional violent deaths such as suicide and homicide; the white squares are unintentional deaths from chart 2 above.)

## 10 Leading Causes of Injury Deaths by Age Group Highlighting Violence-Related Injury Deaths, United States – 2014

| Rank | <1 | 1-4 | 5-9 | 10-14 | 15-24 | 25-34 | 35-44 | 45-54 | 55-64 | 65+ | Total |
|---|---|---|---|---|---|---|---|---|---|---|---|
| 1 | Unintentional Suffocation 991 | Unintentional Drowning 388 | Unintentional MV Traffic 345 | Unintentional MV Traffic 384 | Unintentional MV Traffic 6,531 | Unintentional Poisoning 9,334 | Unintentional Poisoning 9,116 | Unintentional Poisoning 11,009 | Unintentional Poisoning 7,013 | Unintentional Fall 27,044 | Unintentional Poisoning 42,032 |
| 2 | Homicide Unspecified 119 | Unintentional MV Traffic 293 | Unintentional Drowning 125 | Suicide Suffocation 225 | Homicide Firearm 3,587 | Unintentional MV Traffic 5,856 | Unintentional MV Traffic 4,308 | Unintentional MV Traffic 5,024 | Unintentional MV Traffic 4,554 | Unintentional MV Traffic 6,373 | Unintentional MV Traffic 33,736 |
| 3 | Homicide Other Spec., Classifiable 83 | Homicide Unspecified 149 | Unintentional Fire/Burn 68 | Homicide Firearm 174 | Suicide Firearm 3,492 | Homicide Firearm 3,260 | Homicide Firearm 2,830 | Suicide Firearm 3,953 | Suicide Firearm 3,910 | Suicide Firearm 5,367 | Unintentional Fall 31,959 |
| 4 | Unintentional MV Traffic 61 | Unintentional Suffocation 120 | Homicide Firearm 58 | Suicide Firearm 115 | Suicide Suffocation 2,270 | Suicide Firearm 2,629 | Suicide Firearm 2,057 | Suicide Suffocation 2,321 | Unintentional Fall 2,558 | Unintentional Unspecified 4,590 | Suicide Firearm 21,334 |
| 5 | Undetermined Suffocation 40 | Unintentional Fire/Burn 117 | Unintentional Other Land Transport 36 | Unintentional Drowning 105 | Unintentional Poisoning 2,010 | Suicide Suffocation 2,402 | Suicide Suffocation 1,835 | Suicide Poisoning 1,795 | Suicide Poisoning 1,529 | Unintentional Suffocation 3,692 | Suicide Suffocation 11,407 |
| 6 | Unintentional Drowning 29 | Unintentional Pedestrian, Other 107 | Unintentional Suffocation 34 | Unintentional Fire/Burn 49 | Unintentional Drowning 507 | Suicide Poisoning 800 | Suicide Poisoning 1,274 | Unintentional Fall 1,340 | Suicide Suffocation 1,509 | Unintentional Poisoning 1,993 | Homicide Firearm 10,945 |
| 7 | Homicide Suffocation 26 | Homicide Other Spec., Classifiable 73 | Unintentional Natural/Environment 22 | Unintentional Other Land Transport 49 | Suicide Poisoning 363 | Undetermined Poisoning 575 | Undetermined Poisoning 637 | Homicide Firearm 1,132 | Undetermined Poisoning 698 | Adverse Effects 1,554 | Suicide Poisoning 6,808 |
| 8 | Unintentional Natural/Environment 17 | Homicide Firearm 47 | Unintentional Pedestrian, Other 18 | Unintentional Suffocation 33 | Homicide Cut/Pierce 314 | Homicide Cut/Pierce 430 | Unintentional Fall 504 | Undetermined Poisoning 820 | Unintentional Suffocation 539 | Unintentional Fire/Burn 1,151 | Unintentional Suffocation 6,580 |
| 9 | Undetermined Unspecified 16 | Homicide Struck by or Against 38 | Homicide Struck by or Against 16 | Unintentional Poisoning 22 | Undetermined Poisoning 229 | Unintentional Drowning 399 | Unintentional Drowning 363 | Unintentional Suffocation 452 | Homicide Firearm 538 | Suicide Poisoning 1,028 | Unintentional Unspecified 5,848 |
| 10 | Unintentional Fire/Burn 15 | Undetermined Natural/Environment 35 | Homicide Unspecified (Tied) 14 | Homicide Cut/Pierce 19 | Unintentional Other Land Transport 177 | Unintentional Fall 285 | Homicide Cut/Pierce 313 | Unintentional Drowning 442 | Unintentional Unspecified 530 | Suicide Suffocation 880 | Unintentional Drowning 3,406 |

What's interesting about that chart is that unlike some media reports on violent crime would have you believe, there isn't a homicidal maniac lurking on every street corner, seeking to stab or shoot to death certain age demographics who cross their path. In a way, what this chart shows is much, much worse.

For one thing, it's alarming and absolutely tragic how many children are murdered, particularly those under the age of four.[22] These victims are usually shot, or assaulted.[23] Although young children are less likely to be victims of violence than adolescents, when they are victims, parents and other caretakers are more likely than acquaintances and strangers to have inflicted the abuse. Data from the FBI indicates that parents were responsible for 60 percent of the abuse reported to the police, and stepparents and boyfriends or girlfriends of parents accounted for 19 percent.[24]

But it gets worse.

Children have a high rate of suicide between the ages of 10 and 14, using suffocation (e.g., hanging) and firearms. And then suicide remains prevalent through adulthood and until the age of 35 (refer back to Chart 1), when diseases begin to set in. So the charts tell an awful and heartbreaking story: In America, a child is far more likely to be killed by someone in their family circle than die from the flu, and as they age, they're more likely to kill themselves. Suicide is the tenth leading cause of death in the U.S. (Note that physician-assisted deaths are not classified as suicides by state law, so they are not classified as suicides by the CDC, either, and thus are not depicted in this data.)

National numbers such as these may seem remote or abstract, but you can drill down even further to see how people in your specific age group die at your state and local levels. For example, according to the CDC, in 2014 Maine had the oldest population in the country.[25] Half of all Maine deaths were due to cancer, heart disease, or lower respiratory diseases. On the opposite end of the spectrum, the youngest population by state in 2014 was Utah, where heart disease, cancer, and accidents were the leading causes of death.[26]

At the local level, how are you most likely to die in your city or county? Most coroners or medical examiners produce an annual report you can obtain online. It will tell you the demographics of death for the county you live in so you can compare it to the CDC data to see how death is particular to your area relative to the rest of the country. The data most often reflects the "abstract" CDC numbers (because local data is what the CDC data is built on), but you may find something about death in your region that is unusual or surprising. Or, you may discover a "heads up" on something to watch out for.

# DEATH FROM ILLNESS & DISEASE

In 1968, a Harvard Medical School committee defined death as irreversible damage to the brain (brain death). This meant that the person was dead when his or her memories and personality (which are functions of the brain) were irretrievably gone. According to the Uniform Declaration of Death Act of 1981 that is recognized by most states, the legal definition of death is: "An individual who has sustained either (1) irreversible cessation of circulatory and respiratory functions, or (2) irreversible cessation of all functions of the entire brain, including the brain stem, is dead. A determination of death must be made in accordance with accepted medical standards."[27]

So if the heart dies and can't pump oxygen through the body, the brain soon follows because a constant oxygen supply is needed by brain cells to survive. When oxygenated blood to the brain is stopped for whatever reason, the neurons are deprived of oxygen, electrical activity in the brain ceases, and the person loses consciousness in roughly ten seconds, though it may take several minutes for the person to die.[28] Why can't the brain cells just be re-oxygenated with medical treatment, and thus be reactivated and revived? If other cell types are interrupted, they can use energy stores to survive. Neurons can't do this because in the absence of oxygen, they quickly run out of reserves and cannot fuel pathways critical to the survival of the cell. (Cardiac muscle cells are similar, and so also suffer injury quickly when lack of oxygenation—hypoxia—occurs.) Like a flame, neurons require almost continuous oxygen to function. Without oxygen, a flame extinguishes, and in brain cells, the flame not only extinguishes, but the candle is also destroyed by complicated chemical imbalances to the point that the brain cells can't function. This is called "reperfusion injury," and in the oxygen-deprived brain cell, calcium that was actively being kept out, flows in, and permanently damages delicate proteins, ensuring they will never again function properly.[29]

So that's the end result, but how does a person ultimately get to that point? For age, illness, and disease-related deaths, the path is usually slow and relatively painless when the body shuts down. With certain kinds of illness or disease, such as cancer, pain is often inevitable. But a painful disease doesn't imply a difficult death, because medication can be administered for comfort. Both palliative and hospice care programs can provide comprehensive pain regimens to achieve this. Palliative care is intended for people with a serious illness. It can be given at any age or stage of an illness, in addition to curative treatment. On the other hand, hospice provides palliative care after curative treatment for the underlying disease is stopped, and it's clear that the person will not survive their illness. Hospice care is usually given when the person has six months or less to live.[30]

For the most part, dying isn't as beautiful and glamorous as it appears in television and the movies. Neurological changes create physiological changes, and when people aren't familiar with how those processes manifest as a person dies, it can be upsetting to witness. For example, if family members have never witnessed a "death rattle" (where saliva pools in the back of the throat, and breathing changes), it can be tremendously distressing and cause the observer to implore medical personnel to "do something," even though it's a natural step in the physiological process, and the person is actually fine. Also, agitation that dying people exhibit isn't usually due to pain, but witnessing it can cause family members to insist on medication for the person. Since pain medication can't be processed efficiently by organs shutting down in a dying body, medication can actually make things worse.

Breathing pattern changes can look alarming and invoke fears that the person will suffocate, when in reality, the dying person may not be experiencing any breathlessness or suffocation at all. Also, pain does not suddenly increase as a person dies, even though families may assume their loved one is in pain when witnessing grimacing or facial tension caused by mental activity, such as dreams or hallucinations. Most restlessness, agitation, moaning, and groaning that accompany terminal delirium are also not pain-based.[31] This is crucial to understand, because family members will otherwise believe their loved one died a horrible death in terrible pain, and convince themselves that their own death will be similar. The reality is that pain does not suddenly develop in the final hours of life when it wasn't previously present or out of control.[32] So the more advance knowledge of the dying process friends and family have, the less stressful it is to watch their loved one go through it because these processes are anticipated, rather than unknown and shocking.

As a person dies, both the brain and body begin to sacrifice areas that are not critical to survival. The neurological changes involved in the dying process can manifest in two different patterns that have been described as the "two roads to death" (see table below).[33] The "usual road" that most people follow is a decreased level of consciousness that leads to coma and death. The "difficult road" that a few people experience manifests as an agitated delirium due to central nervous system excitation, with or without muscle spasms, and eventually leads to coma and death.[34]

| Routine Dying Process ("Usual Road") | Difficult Dying Process ("Difficult Road") |
|---|---|
| Normal | Normal |
| Sleepy | Restless |
| Lethargic | Confused |
| Semi-responsive | Tremors or quivering |
| Semi-comatose | Hallucinations |
| Comatose | Mumbling delirium |
| ...and finally Death | Involuntary muscle jerking or spasms |
| | Seizures |
| | Semi-comatose |
| | Comatose |
| | ...and finally Death |

Below are the basic signs and symptoms of the body's shutting down processes, which end when all physical systems stop functioning.[35] It's usually an orderly, non-dramatic, and progressive series of physical changes that aren't medical emergencies requiring invasive interventions. These physical changes are the normal, natural way the body prepares itself to die, and most medical responses to them are to ensure comfort, rather than stop their occurrence.[36] Each person is different, so the signs and symptoms, and order in which they occur, will vary.

- The process starts when hunger and thirst decrease or cease in order to conserve energy normally used for digestion, and to prepare the body for complete shut down. Wasting away is common.

- The mouth and lips become dry or parched.

- Slow, prolonged breathing happens first. Then, breathing patterns later change to rapid, shallow breathing or panting due to internal circulation changes.

- Cool skin (especially in the hands and feet) that may turn color is a sign that the circulatory system is shutting down. Blood circulation to the body's extremities decreases in order to conserve it for the most vital organs.

- Metabolism changes cause increasing drowsiness, the person sleeps most of the time, and eventually becomes unrousable.

The following phases can alarm family members because the outer symptoms create the impression that their loved one is in pain. In most cases, the person is not suffering or distressed at all.

- Congestion, or loud gurgling or rattling sounds coming from the person's chest or throat is due to decreased fluid intake, and an inability to cough up normal secretions. This isn't due to pain, and the dying person is usually not aware of them.

- Restless, involuntary, and repetitive motions (such as writhing, or pulling at clothing) occur due to decreased oxygen circulation to the brain, and metabolism changes. Groaning or grimacing are often mistaken for pain.

- Disorientation due to metabolism changes causes confusion about time, place, and identity of medical staff, or family and friends.

- Incontinence occurs due to muscle relaxation and weakness, which can cause loss of bladder and bowel control.

- Decreased urine production is caused by lowered fluid intake, and less blood circulation through the kidneys. It can also include kidney failure.

- The person becomes more withdrawn from and unresponsive to surroundings, and may seem in a comatose-like state. Speech and vision are usually lost, the person drifts in and out of consciousness, and gradually becomes much less responsive to touch or voice.

- Hallucinations occur due to chemical changes in the dying brain. The person may speak to people who have already died, or see places or hear things others can't.

Some people become more alert just before death due to a surge of neurochemicals being released in different parts of the brain as it dies.[37] Stories abound of people who have bursts of energy or hyperawareness after a previously near-comatose state. They suddenly sit up and talk or laugh normally, sometimes giving family members false hope for recovery, and then die soon after.

When death finally occurs, signs include: no response, no heartbeat or breathing, eyes open with pupils enlarged and fixed on a certain spot without blinking, the jaw and mouth slacked open slightly, and bladder and bowel release.

What specifically happens to the body, and how exactly does it feel while dying from certain illnesses, accidents, or diseases? Below are vivid and detailed descriptions of the most common ways to die according to CDC data. Keep in mind death's common denominator: At some point, when the heart can no longer pump blood to all of the organs, and particularly the brain, the brain cells will die. When this happens, the brain can't control the rest of the body, and death occurs. Cells die at different rates, but brain cell death from lack of oxygen, and a heart attack from lack of blood flow to the heart, take only a few minutes to kill.[38] Clinical death occurs when the heart stops beating and the person stops breathing, and can be reversed if the person can be successfully resuscitated. Biological death, which is permanent and irreversible, occurs when cells die due to lack of oxygen, approximately four to six minutes after clinical death.[39]

The point of the descriptions is not to be excessively gruesome or gory—it's to help understand the processes rationally, and decrease the inherent fear of their occurrence.

## Heart Attack & Cardiac Arrest

### What it is:

Cardiac arrest occurs when the electrical impulses of the heart are disrupted. This causes the heartbeat to stop entirely, or causes irregular heart beats known as arrhythmia, which make the electrical impulses in the heart become rapid (ventricular tachycardia) or chaotic (ventricular fibrillation), or both. Without medical aid (such as defibrillation, which uses an electronic device that sends an electric shock to the heart to restore normal heart rhythm), the person will die.[40] Cardiac arrest is not a heart attack, but can occur during a heart attack.

A heart attack (myocardial infarction) is a circulation "plumbing" problem that happens when the blood flow to the heart is blocked.[41] Heart attacks occur when there is a blockage in one or more of the arteries to the heart, preventing the heart from receiving enough oxygen-rich blood. If the heart can't get oxygen, it becomes damaged.

**What it does:**

If the heart is debilitated and can't pump oxygen-rich blood to the brain and other vital organs, death occurs. The person loses consciousness in roughly ten seconds, and can die within minutes without medical aid.

**How it feels:**

**Heart attack** – Symptoms include sweating and increased heart rate as the brain signals that there's a problem. Other symptoms can include nausea and vomiting, difficulty breathing, dizziness, weakness, chest pain, radiating pain in the left arm or between the shoulder blades, and an aching jaw. Heart attack patients say that the pain they experienced was like a clamp squeezing their chest, and it can last from several minutes to many hours. The chest pain is caused when heart muscle dies from oxygen deprivation. In some cases, a heart attack can lead to sudden cardiac arrest, and possibly death.[42]

**Cardiac arrest** – Cardiac arrest often occurs without prior symptoms. There can be a feeling of abnormal heartbeat or shortness of breath. There also may be lightheadedness before the person loses consciousness, collapses, breathing stops, and the person becomes unresponsive. Chest pain can occur as heart muscle dies from lack of oxygen. Without medical attention, the person dies from either not enough oxygenated blood pumped to the rest of the body, or a heart that stopped beating and won't restart. In both cases, if the heart stops beating entirely, brain cells will die within three to seven minutes, and death follows shortly thereafter.[43]

# Cancer

<u>What it is:</u>

Cancer is a malignant growth, or tumors resulting from the uncontrolled division of abnormal cells. It can invade nearby tissues and spread to other parts of the body through the blood and lymph systems.

There are several types of cancer:[44]

- Carcinoma is a cancer that begins in the skin, or in tissues that line or cover internal organs.

- Sarcoma is a cancer that begins in bone, cartilage, fat, muscle, blood vessels, or other connective or supportive tissue.

- Leukemia is a cancer that starts in blood-forming tissue such as bone marrow, and causes large numbers of abnormal blood cells to be produced and enter the bloodstream.

- Lymphoma and multiple myeloma are cancers that begin in the cells of the immune system.

- Central nervous system cancers are cancers that begin in the tissues of the brain and spinal cord.

Staging (I through IV) is a way of describing the size of a cancer and how far it has grown.

**What it does:**

Malignant cancer cells attack tissues or organs, and spread by releasing cells into the bloodstream, allowing them to settle in another area of the body. Cancer generally kills by stopping particular organs or entire physiological systems from working.

As people succumb to cancer, increased weakness makes normal tasks difficult (such as walking), resulting in increased dependence on others. Appetite decreases and weight loss occurs (wasting). The body begins to shut down, and focuses on the organs most necessary for survival, such as the brain, heart, and lungs. Then the dying process (described earlier as the "two roads") begins.

**How it feels:**

About half of all patients who die from any form of cancer experience severe pain at some point. The severity of pain depends on the form of cancer, and its location. Bone pain (the most common type of cancer pain) is caused by tumors pressing on or growing within bone. Tumors that press against nerves cause a burning sensation. Basically, cancer eats away at internal tissues and cells, causing pain by affecting the nerves within them.[45] Cancer treatments such as radiation and chemotherapy can also cause painful nerve damage. Hospice and palliative care helps most cancer patients die a comfortable death by using medication to assist with pain and symptom management.[46]

# Pneumonia & Lower Respiratory Infection

## What it is:

Pneumonia is a lung infection affecting the lung's tiny lung air sacs (alveoli), where oxygenation of the blood occurs. Pneumonia can have many different causes, but the most common are bacteria, viruses, and fungi. In addition to pneumonia, other lower respiratory infections that can kill are acute bronchitis (inflammation) and bronchiolitis (inflammation and infection), influenza, and whooping cough. They infect the lung's airways, obstruct breathing, and prevent oxygenation in the body.[47]

Bacterial pneumonia can worsen without treatment, causing breathing problems, and possibly death. Or, the infection can spread to other areas of the body. Pus or extra fluid may collect in the space around the lungs, damaging them. Or the lungs may be too inflamed and damaged to get enough oxygen, which can damage other body organs, such as the kidneys, heart, and brain, causing death.

Elderly people are at high risk of getting pneumonia; it's the third leading killer of people over age 65 in the U.S.[48] One reason is that they often have other underlying health issues—such as heart disease, other lung diseases such as emphysema, or a weakened immune system—that compound the problem. This makes people less responsive to treatment, and less able to cope with the stress pneumonia places on the organs, which can create lethal complications.[49]

**What it does:**

Respiratory infections make it difficult for oxygen to reach the bloodstream, harming cells and organs. It also causes an increase in the waste gas carbon dioxide in blood levels, which is normally removed by exhalation. Respiratory failure happens when the capillaries in the lung air sacs can't properly exchange carbon dioxide for oxygen.[50]

**How it feels:**

Pneumonia can feel as mild as persistent shortness of breath, or an intense sensation of suffocation. Sharp chest pain can make breathing painful. Without treatment, oxygen levels can plummet to life-threatening levels. If the heart and brain don't get enough oxygen, confusion, coma, heart failure, and eventually death can result.[51] Death from pneumonia can also be caused by inflammation and extensive bleeding in the lungs, which causes breathing to stop.[52]

# Stroke

**What it is:**

Stroke occurs when blood flow to an area of the brain is cut off. When this happens, brain cells are deprived of oxygen and die. The two most common types of stroke are *ischemic* and *hemorrhagic*. An ischemic stroke occurs when an artery carrying blood to the brain becomes blocked, usually by a blood clot. The affected part of the brain then becomes deprived of oxygen-rich blood, and will stop functioning, and the brain tissue will die. Ischemic strokes account for more than 80 percent of all strokes.[53] This type of stroke is sometimes called a "brain attack," because the problem is caused by blockage or clotting, similar to a heart attack.

Hemorrhagic strokes occur when when a blood vessel in the brain ruptures or leaks, spilling blood into the surrounding tissues. The pressure from the leaked blood causes the brain to swell inside the skull, and damages brain cells and tissue.   There are two types of hemorrhagic strokes: *Intracerebral hemorrhage* is the most common type, and occurs when an artery in the brain bursts, flooding the surrounding brain tissue with blood. *Subarachnoid hemorrhage* is less common, and occurs when there is bleeding in the area between the brain and the thin tissues that cover it.[54]

### What it does:

The effects of a stroke depend on where it occurs in the brain, and how much of the brain is damaged.[55] When brain cells die during a stroke, abilities controlled by that area of the brain (such as memory and muscle control) are lost.[56]

### How it feels:

Unlike heart attacks and their subsequent chest pain, strokes are often painless, with less than one-third of patients experiencing pain. Hemorrhagic strokes such as aneurysms are more likely than ischemic strokes to cause pain, and tend to manifest as a sudden and severe headache.[57]

Most people die peacefully after a major stroke, without any pain or discomfort. Some strokes are severe enough to cause cause immediate coma. Death occurs when the brain can't keep the body breathing or circulation flowing.[58] Most comatose stroke patients die within days or weeks of their stroke. Many stroke deaths are not due to direct effects on the brain; they are caused by complications from secondary infections, such as pneumonia, urinary infections, or blood clots impacting the lungs (pulmonary embolism) that occur before the patient has had a chance to fully recover from the stroke.[59]

# DEATHS FROM ACCIDENTS & VIOLENCE

Just like lingering deaths due to illness or disease, accidental and violent deaths are ultimately caused by the same recurring mechanics of death: lack of circulation by the heart, which creates a lack of oxygen to the brain, which then causes death. Accidents and violence are really just variations on how quickly death occurs, and the amount of pain involved.

Even when a death is expected—such as those due to illness or disease—the survivors still feel shock and disbelief. But both of those feelings are greatly intensified when a death is due to an accident or violence, because the survivors often feel they were robbed of their loved one "before their rightful time."

Despite the huge amount of progress in emergency medical services and trauma systems, pre-hospital care, injury prevention, and automotive safety, the proportion of deaths occurring immediately after injury has remained unchanged at 50 to 60 percent since studies were first conducted on the subject in the 1970s. In other words, humans are still as vulnerable as ever to the devastating nature of injures to the central nervous and cardiovascular systems, despite advances in technology and practices.[60]

# Drowning

## What occurs:

Water in the lungs causes death by preventing breathing overall, and lack of oxygenation to both heart and lung tissue specifically, causing death. Circulatory and respiratory failure occurs simultaneously. The heart either quivers uselessly (ventricular fibrillation) or irregularly (arrhythmia), unable to pump and circulate blood. Death can occur in three to five minutes.[61]

Drownings occur most frequently on weekends (40%), in the summertime months (May through August), in rural areas, and in the southern and western U.S. (62%). In California, Arizona, and Florida, drowning is the number one cause of injury-related death.[62]

## How it feels:

When victims submerge, they hold their breath for a minute or two before inevitably inhaling water, which triggers the airway to seal shut. [63] According to survivors, there is a burning or tearing sensation in the chest as water eventually fills the lungs.[64] A feeling of calmness or tranquility soon arises, as oxygen deprivation and carbon dioxide retention cause the person to lose consciousness. Cardiac arrest ensues, and finally, brain death.[65] Death usually occurs within four to eight minutes of complete submersion.[66]

# Hanging

## What occurs:

Hanging is a type of strangulation caused by a noose (ligature) around the neck that puts pressure on internal structures (such as the larynx, trachea, pharynx, and epiglottis). This causes suffocation by pinching off the airway and creating a lack of oxygen in the body. It simultaneously pinches off the carotid artery, cutting off blood flow to the brain. Unconsciousness usually starts in ten seconds. Pressure on the neck can harm nerves that supply the heart (vagal inhibition) and create arrhythmia (irregular heartbeat) and cardiac arrest.[67]

Hanging is the second most common form of suicide in the U.S. (firearm-based suicides are number one), accounting for approximately 25 percent of all suicides.[68] More than half of hanging victims are under 45 years old, and the majority of them are males. A history of drug or alcohol abuse is common among the victims, as is psychiatric illness.[69]

## How it feels:

Death by hanging is most frequently due to asphyxia and hypoxia caused by airway and blood flow blockages. The resulting oxygen deprivation causes unconsciousness and eventual death.[70] Death by hanging is usually rapid if the cervical vertebrae are broken or dislocated, which can initiate cardiac arrest. Asphyxia and hypoxia deaths from hanging are a little slower; it can take between three to five minutes for the person to die.[71]

The first symptoms of approaching death from hanging are flashes of light and ringing and hissing noises in the ears. Mental confusion sets in, rendering the person helpless to stop their predicament. Convulsions arise with violent struggling, the face distorts, causing the eyes to bulge, and breathing ceases. Loss of consciousness ensues quickly enough to consider hanging to be a painless death.[72]

# Gunshot Wounds

## What occurs:

Depending on the gun's caliber and the area of the body that was shot, if the bullet hits a vital organ, death can be instant. Gunshot wounds to the head are the most lethal of all firearm injuries, with an estimated fatality rate greater than 90 percent. Gunshot wounds to the heart have fatality rates close to 80 percent.[73] Thankfully, only 30 percent of firearm injuries in the U.S. are fatal.[74]

When a bullet enters the body, tissue is crushed, and numerous factors influence its path and the magnitude of subsequent injuries. Structures that are less dense that have elasticity may sustain less damage than structures with greater density and more rigidity. For example, lung tissue has low density with high elasticity, and tends to be less damaged than muscle with higher density and some elasticity. The liver, spleen, brain, and adipose tissue have little elasticity, and are easily injured. Organs that are fluid-filled, such as the bladder, heart, major blood vessels and bowel, may rupture due to pressure waves—even without direct contact by the bullet.[75]

The bullet may deform or fragment, tearing and crushing tissue, and contact more than one bone or organ, or damage major blood vessels. Bones readily break and fragment when struck by a bullet, and the fragments can severely damage internal organs, such as a rib fragment displacing into a lung, puncturing and collapsing it. The main concern with gunshot wounds that involve the intestine or stomach isn't bleeding, but infections that result from the contents spilling from those organs into the abdominal cavity.[76]

### How it feels:

The most immediate and damaging effect of a gunshot wound is usually severe bleeding, with the likelihood of hypovolemic shock (inadequate delivery of oxygen to vital organs, which become damaged and die).[77] The most important factors affecting survival odds are the location of the injury, the amount of blood lost, and how quickly the victim can get to a hospital.[78] Skin, muscle, and bone are all severely damaged by bullets, which shred bone and organs, disintegrate into shrapnel, and ricochet inside the body. This damages nerves and creates an excruciating internal burning sensation. If the victims bleeds to death, they will lose consciousness before succumbing.

# Fire

### What occurs:

Fumes and poison gases are the biggest killers in fires,

long before heat and flames reach their victims. Most fire deaths are due to inhalation of carbon monoxide and other products of combustion (such as cyanide), combined with suffocation from lack of oxygen. Roughly 40 percent of house fire victims are overcome by toxic gases and fumes while still sleeping.[79] Incineration of the body follows.

### How it feels:

Burns inflict immediate and intense pain through stimulation of the nerves in the skin—a horrific agony until the person goes into shock and loses consciousness. The pain is so intense because the burns trigger a rapid inflammatory response, which boosts sensitivity to pain in the injured tissues and surrounding areas.[80] The fire rapidly burns through soft tissue such as the skin, which shrinks, blisters and splits open, releasing fat. Muscle begins to char, flexing and extending limbs as they tighten and shrink. Internal organs are then destroyed by the heat or flames.[81]

Most people don't die instantly from burns, however. More than half of deaths occur within the first 48 hours from secondary shock due to fluid loss from burned skin surfaces.[82] Blood poisoning, bacterial infections, and gangrene from the burns also kill people within a few days after the fire.

# Bombing or Explosion

### What occurs:

Though terrorism is certainly a factor, the reality is that most explosive or blast injuries are caused by commercial or industrial accidents, such as gas explosions.[83] A person can be killed by an explosion in several ways:[84]

- The person can be blown to pieces if they are in close proximity to the blast.

- Severe, lethal injury can be incurred from the air pressure generated by the shock wave.

- Fatal "flash" burns exceeding 3000 degrees Fahrenheit can occur from the heat generated by the blast; or regular burns can occur if clothing catches fire.

- The person can be struck and killed by shrapnel or flying debris propelled by the explosion.

- The body can be crushed and killed by debris from buildings demolished by an explosion.

- The person can be overcome by toxic fumes and gases created by the blast.

Blast injuries are categorized in four different ways:[85]

- Primary injuries are caused by the direct effect of blast overpressure on tissue.

- Secondary injuries are caused by flying objects that strike people.

- Tertiary injuries are caused by high-energy explosions that fling people through the air and they strike other objects.

- Quaternary injuries encompass all other injuries caused by explosions.

More than one factor can affect a blast victim's survival rate, such as the type of detonation, and the victim's distance from the center of the explosion. Mortality is higher when explosions occur in closed or confined spaces.[86]

<u>**How it feels:**</u>

Shockwaves can pass through solid tissue like muscles and the liver, causing little or no damage, but can devastate air-filled tissue such as the lungs, bowel, and the middle ear. "Blast lung" is the most common fatal injury that strikes initial survivors of the shock wave.[87] Organs surrounded by fluid-filled cavities (e.g., the brain and spinal cord) are particularly susceptible to primary blast injury.[88] Internal perforation and hemorrhaging usually occur, even if there are no obvious external wounds. Brain injury can also occur with no outward signs of damage.

When people are either hit by debris, or physically flung into other objects such as a wall or vehicle by the blast wave, both penetrating and blunt trauma injuries can occur. Penetrating trauma occurs when an object pierces the skin and enters a tissue of the body, creating an open wound. In blunt, or non-penetrating trauma, there may be an impact and subsequent damage, but the skin is not necessarily broken.[89]

# Stabbing

<u>**What occurs:**</u>

A stab wound can either be minor or fatal, depending on the body region that is cut. It can cause internal and external bleeding that leads to shock (massive loss of blood that prevents oxygenation), but chances of survival are good if the stab wound doesn't affect major blood vessels, get infected, or damage vital organs. Most deaths from stab wounds are usually due to organ failure or blood loss.

Large knives require strong force to penetrate skin, and the knife tip can get snagged on clothing. Cheap kitchen knives tend to bend and break on impact, and if the knife tip strikes bone, the tip can break off and remain embedded in the bone.[90] Stab wounds caused by tools such as screwdrivers, chisels and ice picks are sometimes mistaken for small caliber gunshot wounds. Unless the victim is incapacitated at the time of the assault, knives are rarely pushed into the body and withdrawn at exactly the same angle. Parts of the torso that compress (such as the chest wall or abdomen), can indent during a knife attack, causing damage to structures deep within that area at a depth that seems beyond the reach of the weapon.[91]

Overhand-style stabbing creates more cutting power through the skin than lateral slashing. Skin provides the greatest resistance to penetration, while strong, secondary resistive forces are provided by muscle. Tissues other than skin (such as ligaments) can offer enough resistance to slow a knife down, requiring the assailant to exert more pressure in order to complete a thrust. Fat gives little resistance.[92]

## How it feels:

Many victims report that a stab wound is often initially unnoticed.[93] Unless the stab wound involves the brainstem, death is not instantaneous. If the heart or major blood vessels are targeted, the assault may be enough to cause the victim to quickly collapse, but not immediately lose consciousness. Victims of stabbing are capable of energetic action—such as running and climbing stairs—before collapsing.[94]

Slit-like stab wounds cause less blood loss, because the wound margins are in close proximity, and the elasticity of the tissues helps to contain the blood flow.[95] The more stab wounds, the greater likelihood of bleeding and organ damage, and the less likelihood of survival.[96]

If a stabbing victim doesn't die instantly or lose consciousness immediately from the stabbing, intense pain will ensue if there's serious internal damage. Seventy percent of stabbing victims capable of action following an assault die within thirty minutes. Most victims with heart *and* major blood vessel injuries die within one hour. Victims incurring a penetrating injury to the heart rarely survive longer than 12 hours.[97]

# Motor Vehicle Accident

<u>**What occurs:**</u>

Two thousand pounds (or more) of metal and combustible material moving at high speeds, and carrying delicate human tissue, is a recipe for disaster should something go wrong—and that's before you factor in impairments from drugs or alcohol. Motor vehicle accidents (which includes cars, motorcycles, etc.) are the leading cause of unintentional injury deaths for most people under age 25, and the second leading cause of of unintentional injury deaths for everyone over age 25.

Now that's a lot of lousy drivers out there. Unsurprisingly, alcohol is involved in one third of all traffic-related deaths in the U.S.[98]

Injuries and circumstances in motor vehicle fatalities can vary widely; drivers, passengers, adults, children, pedestrians, bicyclists, and motorcycle riders all incur a range of patterns and types of injuries. Common ways for vehicle occupants to die from a motor vehicle accident include: from the impact of what they hit, such as another vehicle; from hitting other objects if they are ejected from the vehicle; or from objects that hit them by intruding into the vehicle upon impact.

Aside from whether the victim(s) were wearing seatbelts or not, death from blunt force trauma caused by the impact is dependent on how fast the vehicle was going, and how solid the object impacted. (Think irresistible force meeting an unmovable object.) A high-speed accident can cause the neck to snap, resulting in instant death. It can also crush the driver into the steering wheel or dashboard, causing massive internal damage and hemorrhaging. Vehicle occupants can be ejected, dismembered, or killed by the car shearing to pieces or crushing. External objects such as concrete barriers, road signs, or trees can also penetrate the interior of the vehicle, harming the occupants by impaling, pinning or crushing them. If the occupants become trapped in the vehicle, fire from the crash can burn them to death.

For pedestrians and cyclists in particular, being hit by any kind of vehicle, especially one at high speed, is often fatal. Pedestrians now account for about 15 percent of all motor vehicle crash-related deaths, up from 11 percent a decade ago.[99] Bicyclists die on U.S. roads at a rate double that of vehicle occupants.[100] Each year about 2 percent of motor vehicle crash deaths are bicyclists. In a majority of bicyclist deaths, the most serious injuries are to the head, highlighting the importance of wearing a bicycle helmet.[101]

### How it feels:

Blunt force trauma is sustained by drivers and passengers when they impact the interior surfaces of the vehicle. While the windshield is often the first thing passengers hit, drivers will also do so after hitting the steering wheel first.[102] Facial and skull fractures are common. If airbags fail to deploy, steering wheel impact can cause extensive internal chest (thoracic) injuries, including rib and sternum fractures, spine fractures, lung bruising, rib fracture-associated punctured lungs, rupture or puncture of the heart, or severing of the aorta.

In a frontal impact, particularly for the driver, the heart and aorta can be crushed between the sternum and spine and rupture, causing severe internal bleeding in the chest cavities, and death from shock can occur.[103] Damage to organs such as the liver, spleen, pancreas and kidneys are common. Severe whiplash to the upper cervical spine can cause devastating injuries to the brainstem or upper cervical cord, causing rapid death.

Temporary ejection, in which an occupant exits a side window briefly in a rollover, but remains in the vehicle when it comes to rest, can fatally crush the skull and torso. In rollover accidents where the vehicle comes to rest on its roof, seatbelted occupants can suffocate in the harness, particularly if they are obese or intoxicated. If a person is completely ejected from the vehicle, it can fully or partially come to rest on top of the victim and crush them to death. Ejection of occupants occurs with greater frequency in rollover accidents and side impacts that cause rotation of the vehicle, and ejection happens seven times more often when the occupant is not restrained by a seatbelt. Fatality rates are much lower for non-ejected occupants compared to ejected occupants in the same crash.[104]

Motor vehicle death statistics include pedestrians hit by vehicles. A pedestrian can be run over by a vehicle, crushing their trunk or limbs and rupturing internal organs. When a pedestrian is thrown onto the hood or windshield, pelvic, spine, skull, and rib fractures—as well as severe internal injuries—can occur. Head and neck injuries are the most common cause of death in pedestrian accidents. Typical blunt force trauma, such as facial and skull fractures, blood leaking in the skull, and cervical fractures, are common. Deadly pedestrian head injuries can also occur when they land on the roadway after being struck by a vehicle.[105]

Collision-related motor vehicle fires represent only three percent of *all* causes of motor vehicle fires, but account for the majority of vehicle fire fatalities. Occupants become trapped in vehicles, or are incapacitated so that they can't escape.[106]

# Electrocution

## What occurs:

Electricity kills by attacking the heart, interrupting its rhythm. Electrocution is normally due to household and industrial accidents. Lightning occasionally strikes people, but the majority of strikes don't result in death.[107]

In the U.S. and Canada, typical household electricity provides 110V (volts) for general use, and 240V for high-powered appliances, while industrial electrical and high-tension power lines can have more than 100,000V. In accidental electrocutions—which usually involve low, household current—the most common cause of death is arrhythmia (improper changes to the heart's normal beating). Higher currents can produce immediate unconsciousness by conducting the current through the brain and the heart.[108] High-voltage direct current (DC) electrocution doesn't last long, because it throws the victim away from the electrical source by causing a powerful, single muscle contraction. However, alternating current (AC) of the same voltage is considered to be far more dangerous than DC, because the cyclic flow of electrons causes continuous involuntary muscle contraction, which makes the victim continue to grip the electrical conduit, prolonging their exposure to the source.

Current passing directly through the body heats tissue and causes electrothermal burns, both to the skin surface and deeper tissues, depending on their resistance. Blood vessels, muscles, and nerves have high electrolyte and water content, which makes them good conductors of electricity—better than bone, fat, and skin.[109]

Electrocution typically causes damage at the source contact point (usually the hands) and the ground contact point (usually the feet).[110]

The odds of getting hit by lightning are roughly 1 in 1.9 million.[111] Lightning bolts can contain millions of volts of electricity, but fatal injuries occur when the body converts the electricity into heat. In most direct strikes, a portion of the current moves just over the skin surface (called flashover) and can produce burns. The other portion of the current moves through the body—usually through the cardiovascular and nervous systems.[112] Similar to other types of electrocution, lightning strike deaths are caused by cardiac arrhythmia and total cessation of heartbeat.[113]

About two thirds of U.S. lightning victims were enjoying outdoor leisure activities before being struck, with water-related activities topping the list. Of the water-related activities, fishing ranked highest, and boating and beach activities also contributed significantly to the water-related deaths.[114]

### How it feels:

High-level currents can kill instantly by stopping the heart upon contact. Or they can kill more slowly by causing the heart to flutter rather than pump (ventricular fibrillation), which stops the heart from carrying oxygen to the rest of the body, particularly the brain. Electrocution also causes burns and leaves visible scarring. Fatal low-level currents don't usually leave an external mark, but can kill within minutes by causing heart arrhythmia (abnormal heart rhythm). Electricity passing through the brain can cause severe neurological problems, such as loss of nervous control, and result in rapid loss of consciousness, and ultimately death.[115]

Burns and traumatic injuries cause the majority of deaths from electrical injuries.[116] Without prolonged unconsciousness or cardiac arrest, a person's chances of recovery from electrocution are excellent.

# Falling

**What occurs:**

Fatalities from falls from heights are dependent on several factors: the height of the fall, the victim's body weight, velocity, the type of surface impacted, the orientation of the body at impact, and the elasticity and viscosity of the part of the body that impacts (e.g., head, feet, side, etc.). As a person falls, acceleration occurs until the person reaches terminal velocity (the fastest speed it can fall in gravity, which is roughly 122 miles per hour). The energy from the speed of the fall is immediately transferred to the body at the moment of impact, causing severe or fatal injuries.[117]

Falls are classified as either from lesser or greater heights. Lesser height falls are falls under 30 feet, and greater height falls are plunges from more than 30 feet. Factors contributing to falls from lesser heights include faulty equipment, such as ladders and scaffold structures, and human factors, such as intoxication and inattention. In occupational settings, the most common type of accident is a fall from a lesser height. In those falls, the brain, spinal cord, and extremities are subject to the worst damage.[118] Two thirds of victims falling from lesser heights die from head trauma. Greater height falls are often suicide attempts, whether from tall buildings or bridges, and deaths result mostly from multiple traumas.[119] The difference in trauma resulting from the two types of falls is that in falls from lesser heights (30 feet or less), the body doesn't have enough time to reposition itself before impact. If you fall head first, you tend to stay that way until impact. In falls from greater heights, a person can tumble into several different positions on the way down.

People have fallen from heights and survived because of the numerous factors that determine whether a fall will be fatal or not. The person may fall on something soft that gives way when they impact (such as loose soil), or they may deflect some of the force of the fall on the way down, such as hitting scaffolding or awnings. The position they land in is also crucial, since people don't always fall in a skydiver's 'X' position, and can land headfirst, which is usually fatal.[120] When landing feet-first, the impact forces the leg joints upward in a shearing action as they are driven past the hip joint. Aside from fractures, in a feet-first landing the femoral artery can be severed, resulting in hemorrhage and death.[121]

### How it feels:

People who incur multiple blunt force injuries and traumas from a fall have the shortest survival times. Instant death occurs in almost half of all falls where multiple trauma occurs, which involves massive bone fractures and massive internal bleeding. In general, the greater the height of the fall, the more multiple and severe the fractures and subsequent internal injuries are.[122] Multiple trauma from falls usually includes bruised, collapsed, or burst lungs, often punctured by broken ribs; and exploded hearts or severed major blood vessels which burst upon impact.[123] Such massive internal hemorrhaging causes shock (blood pressure too low to pump oxygenated blood throughout the body), and rapid death. Most fall victims die in the first few seconds or minutes after landing.[124]

Head trauma causes instant death in one third of falling victims. The skull can simply break open, scattering brain matter. Or severe head injuries can occur, such as multiple skull fractures, ruptures of brain structures, and severe bleeding within the skull.[125] If a person doesn't die immediately from impact, multiple organ failure due to infections in the blood that disrupt flow to the organs (sepsis), or lung arteries that become clotted (pulmonary embolism) can kill the victim soon after the fall.[126]

# Drug Overdose

**What occurs:**

Depending on the drug used, respiratory and heart failure are the most common causes of most overdose deaths. Opioids (such as heroin, and painkillers like fentanyl or hydrocodone) cause low blood pressure and low heart rate, reducing the brain's responsiveness to changes in carbon dioxide levels and lack of oxygen (respiratory depression). In fatal cases, the victim stops breathing.[127]

One out of every four drug overdose deaths in 2015 involved heroin.[128] A lifesaving anti-overdose drug (Naloxone) blocks the effects of opioid drugs. If given soon enough, Naloxone can counter overdose effects usually within minutes, and buy the victim time until more advanced medical assistance can be administered.[129]

Methamphetamine can cause heart failure in the short term, with liver, kidney, and lung damage potentially fatal in the long run. During a methamphetamine overdose, blood pressure can also plummet to fatal levels and lead to heart failure. Overdose from antipsychotic drugs, anticonvulsant agents, ethanol, and other sedative hypnotic agents can induce coma, but respiratory depression consistent with other forms of overdose is usually absent.[130]

Outer symptoms of overdose include little to no breathing; blue or purple lips or fingernails; limpness; vomiting or gurgling; and unresponsiveness.[131]

### How it feels:

Instantaneous death is rare. An overdose is characterized by slowed breathing and heart rate, and a loss of consciousness before respiratory failure sets in, killing the victim. The predominant cause of death from opioid overdoses is respiratory failure. Less common are acute lung injury, life-threatening seizures, and heart damage.[132]

Painkillers and sleeping pills are most commonly used for suicide attempts. The pills relax the muscles in the throat and interfere with breathing, or cause sleep apnea, a form of breathing obstruction. The overdose victim dies within a few minutes from lack of oxygen in the lungs.[133]

# AUTOPSY

Autopsy means "to see for oneself," and is performed when there are suspicious circumstances surrounding a person's death, or when there are no indications of natural causes. Autopsies are conducted by either coroners or medical examiners, and there are significant differences between the two. Coroners can be elected or appointed. Many coroners aren't doctors, and some work in fields that may not even be related to the position (e.g., sheriff, local business owner). In the event that a non-medical coroner needs an autopsy performed, they can have the body sent to a medical examiner for determination of death.[134] Medical examiners are doctors, but they may not be forensic pathologists trained in death investigation.

So why is there such a discrepancy in qualifications between the two throughout the country? In short: money. In many rural regions, there may not be any qualified forensic pathologists, or the proper facilities needed for them to do their jobs. Also, if rural areas have little to no violent crime or unexplainable deaths, a full-time forensic pathologist isn't needed—the job can be outsourced to a larger, more appropriate facility in a nearby county if necessary.[135]

Qualifications aside, the coroner and medical examiner do share some of the same core responsibilities, including identifying the body, notifying the next of kin, collecting and returning personal items found on the body to the deceased's family, and signing death certificates.

Forensic pathologists perform autopsies to determine a person's specific cause of death by deeply examining the corpse, because a person can die from multiple things, or have the actual cause masked by something else. For example, a person can succumb to cardiac arrest while driving, and then appear to be killed by blunt force injuries when their car crashes. Or, a person can be killed in a motor vehicle crash, but the medical examiner needs to do an autopsy to see if alcohol was in the victim's blood at the time of the accident. Even in hospitals with sophisticated diagnostic methods and technology, the diagnosis of a disease or the cause of death is wrong in an estimated ten to fifteen percent of cases. It takes an autopsy to determine the true cause of death—otherwise, the truth of what occurred will be buried or cremated along with the deceased.

# CHAPTER SIX

# YOU'RE DEAD. NOW WHAT?

When the brain stops functioning, it loses all ability to keep the other systems working properly. Several different processes then occur simultaneously.

Somatic death is the death of the body as a whole, and occurs before the death of the individual organs, cells, and parts of cells. Somatic death can be difficult to determine, because the symptoms of transitional states (such as a comas), can mimic the signs of death. Signs of somatic death include: no heartbeat; breathing stops; pupils enlarge and the eyes may remain open and fixated; skin color pales once blood circulation stops; body temperature cools; muscles relax, releasing of urine and/or feces; the jaw slacked open; and fluids gurgling as they settle internally. Organs of the body die at different rates. Although brain cells can survive up to five minutes after somatic death, heart cells can live for approximately 15 minutes, and kidney cells for approximately 30 minutes. This is why organs can be donated and transplanted.[1]

The human body is composed of approximately 64 percent water, 20 percent protein, 10 percent fat, 1 percent of carbohydrate, and 5 percent minerals, and disintegration begins rapidly after a person dies.

## PHYSICAL STAGES OF DECOMPOSITION[2]

| Number of Days Since Death – Phase | Physical Action | Bugs: The Cleaning Crew |
|---|---|---|
| 1 – Fresh phase | Immediately after death, the following stages begin within the first few minutes, and continue for hours afterward: *Pallor mortis* (skin pales due to lack of blood circulation) begins after the heart stops beating. *Algor mortis* (body cooling) follows since normal body temperature cannot be internally maintained anymore. *Rigor Mortis* (skeletal muscle stiffening) begins 5 to 10 hours after death, and disappears a few days later. *Livor mortis* (pooling of blood to the underside of body) begins a couple hours after death and peaks 8 to 12 hours later. | Flies and other carrion insects arrive and lay eggs in all open orifices, such as the mouth, wounds, etc. |

| | | |
|---|---|---|
| 1 – Fresh phase (cot'd) | Cell death (autolysis) begins. The body's own bacteria and enzymes consume tissue, creating skin and internal organ blistering. | |
| 4 – Bloating phase | The accumulation of gases within the body causes a bloated appearance. Blisters burst, releasing fluid that loosens skin layers. | Maggots hatch, consuming body fluids and soft tissue such as skin. |
| 14 – Active decay phase | The corpse loses the most mass due to the heavy feeding of maggots and the release of decomposition fluids into the surrounding environment. Liquefaction of tissues and disintegration are very apparent, and strong odors persist. | Beetles eat some of the maggots and firmer body tissues, such as ligaments. |
| 30 – Advanced decay phase | The body deflates from release of the gases that caused the bloating, and collapses into itself as insects consume the remaining tissue. | Bacteria and insects continue consuming, digesting, and releasing tissue proteins, but slower than before. |

| Number of Days Since Death – Phase | Physical Action | Bugs: The Cleaning Crew |
|---|---|---|
| 60 – Skeletonization dry/ remains phase | As the last flesh and hair is consumed, the body dries out and insects leave only the bones, stripped clean. | Mites, moths, and other small insects eat hair, nails, etc., until only the skeleton remains. |

There are five stages of decomposition—the overall processes of breaking down the entire organism—that are catalyzed by two chemical processes which break down the body: 1) *Autolysis*, which is the breaking down of tissues by the body's own internal chemicals and enzymes; and 2) *Putrefaction*, the individual destruction of the body tissues, and its liquefaction through bacteria.[3]

Why do bones last so long, considering how rapidly the rest of the corpse decomposes? Bone is initially very resistant to destruction, but it eventually breaks, decalcifies and dissolves. How fast this happens depends on the soil, water, and flora and wildlife in the immediate environment. Acidic soils (such as those found in forests) dissolve bones faster than alkaline soils (such as those found in deserts). Bacteria and fungi also have an effect because they can penetrate bone and release the minerals into the environment. Animals also eat bones, and can move them from a gravesite. And plant roots attracted to bone minerals such as calcium and phosphorus can wrap around and split or fracture bones.

Unless preserved or even mummified in some way, bodies disintegrate following the processes above. However, rates of decomposition are affected by how much protection a corpse has from the elements. Burial in a coffin slows the process tremendously; and even the type of soil a body is buried in can make a difference. Coarse textured soils with low moisture content frequently promote desiccation (drying out), which can inhibit decomposition and result in the natural preservation of a corpse for thousands of years.[4] A body wrapped in blankets, or buried in a shallow grave, will be much less exposed than a naked corpse laying on the ground. Protected bodies also decompose slower because insects can't easily access them.[5]

Watery graves are unique because the decomposition rate of a corpse submerged in water is dependent on several factors. The decomposition rate in water is usually much slower than a grave in the ground because of low temperatures and low levels of oxygen, unless the corpse can float to the surface and insect colonization can occur.[6] Putrefaction also occurs more slowly in water than in air, and more rapidly in warm, fresh water than in cold, saltwater. Decay is also more rapid in stagnant water than in running water.[7]

Putrefaction is delayed when a body is submerged in deep water and protected by clothing. Once the body is recovered from the water, putrefaction is hastened. The skin of the hands and feet becomes swollen, bleached, and wrinkled after immersion. After several weeks in water, flesh is softened enough to be stripped away by currents or contact with floating objects. Fish or other sea life (crabs, shrimps, etc.) may also consume the remains.[8]

# CHAPTER SEVEN

# NEXT STEPS FOR SURVIVORS

If you're an organ donor, your physician or hospice should be alerted just before death. Vital organs perish quickly, but tissues such as bone, skin, heart valves, and corneas can be donated within the first 24 hours of death[1] If you haven't requested organ donation, or donated the body to a medical school (which will make prearrangements), a physician doesn't need to attend. A naturally-occurring death is not an emergency. There is usually no need to call medical personnel immediately. Many people find it comforting to spend some time with their now-deceased loved one, seeing them finally at peace.[2]

Some arrangements can't be done in advance, however. Steps to be taken shortly after a person dies include: obtaining a pronouncement of death form from authorized medical personnel; transferring the body from the place of death to a funeral home; making funeral arrangements; applying for a burial permit if needed (check your local laws); and obtaining death certificates.[3]

As soon as possible, the death must be officially pronounced by authorized medical personnel such as a doctor. This person also fills out the forms certifying the cause, time, and place of death. This makes it possible for an official death certificate to be prepared, which will be needed to settle the deceased's estate. If the person died in a hospital, medical personnel will complete the pronouncement of death form. Federal law mandates that the person completing the pronouncement of death form must notify the hospital's organ procurement staff, who will offer the family one last chance to donate organs or tissue.[4] Hospital staff can then arrange for the body to be transferred to a funeral provider or other designated facility. In some cases, the doctor may ask if you want an autopsy. (Physical signs of an autopsy are usually hidden by clothing if you're having a funeral with viewing). If you consent, after the autopsy is complete, the body will be released to the funeral provider.

Similar to hospitals, deaths that occur in nursing homes have on-staff medical professionals authorized to complete the pronouncement of death form. Since most nursing homes require the identification of a funeral establishment as part of their pre-admission procedures, nursing home staff can also arrange transport of the body to the pre-designated funeral home.

When a person dies at home, there is no need to move the body right away, but the physician who will complete the pronouncement of death form must be notified. This doesn't have to be done at the moment of death or immediately after, but before the body can be moved, the form must be completed. If hospice or palliative care was involved, they can complete the form.

If not, call 9-1-1 for them to dispatch medical personnel. If it appears that the death was not from natural causes, the coroner's office will be contacted to see if an autopsy needs to be done.[5] Once family members are ready, and the pronouncement of death form is complete, the designated funeral home can be called to remove the body. Most funeral homes are available 24/7 and respond quickly.

If the person dies in a different state than where they reside, or if they die while out of the country, there are additional steps that need to be taken.[6] A local funeral home can coordinate arrangements with a funeral home where the person died.

If a death was due to an accident or crime, the person may be pronounced dead at the scene by the responding medical examiner. Or, the body may be transported to a hospital or a coroner's office to be declared dead on arrival (DOA) there, and an autopsy will be performed to determine the cause of death.[7]

After the pronouncement of death form is complete, and the body has been removed, inform other physicians or specialists who worked with the deceased. Also, cancel any medical services and return medical equipment (such as oxygen tanks, etc.) to their providers.

Within a few days after death, the focus shifts to arranging the funeral, and initiating settlement of the estate.

# BURIAL & OTHER OPTIONS

If advanced planning was done, the deceased's family will be aware of funeral and burial wishes; otherwise, they'll have to search to see if there was a prepaid burial plan. If not, they can contact a funeral home and make arrangements. They can then submit an obituary to the local newspaper (check their deadlines), and post news of the death on the requisite social media outlets.

If the person was in the military, belonged to a fraternal order, or was a member of a church, survivors can contact those organizations to have them conduct funeral services (some even provide burial benefits). A friend or relative can keep an eye on the deceased's home, take care of pets, collect mail, clean, and water plants.

Funerals are a social event for the living to get closure and support, and cultural and religious beliefs generally determine what the final disposition of the body will be. Many state laws require human remains to be disposed of by burial, cremation, or donation to science (or else a burial permit won't be issued), but the full range of options include:

- Burial (land or sea)

- Cremation

- Mummification

- Cryonics (deep-freezing)

- Promession (freeze-dried and composted)

- Donation for scientific research

For burial at sea, the Environmental Protection Agency (EPA) has strict laws that must be complied with. Professional companies such as the Neptune Society can be hired to make lawful arrangements.[8] At the state level, scattering of cremated remains in lakes, rivers or other inland waters is not subject to federal regulation, but states may have their own laws for burial in inland waters, or prohibit it entirely. Contact your state environmental board, public health agency, or mortuary board to determine any legal requirements that apply.

Cremation involves exposing the body to temperatures between 1400 and 1800 degrees Fahrenheit in a furnace (retort) for a few hours. Once the remains have cooled, they are sifted to remove any metals (such as fillings, or medical pins and plates), and then placed in a pulverizer to grind the remaining bone fragments into a consistent ash. (The term "ashes" is a bit misleading, since what families receive after cremation isn't a soft powder, but a grayish, coarse, fine, gravel-like material of the ground-up remains of bones.) The cremated remains are then returned to the deceased's family. An average human body takes from two to three hours to burn completely, and will produce an average of three to nine pounds of ash.[9]

If you have a spare $67,000, and fancy a traditional Egyptian burial, mummification may be just the ticket. Summum, a Utah-based, tax-exempt organization that is the world's only mummification company, mummifies people (and their pets). In their version of mummification, the organs are taken out and cleansed, and the body is submerged in a tank to hydrate for more than 70 days. Afterward, the body is covered with lanolin and wax, followed by layers of cotton gauze and a fiberglass finish. The body is then encased in a steel or bronze casket. The process takes 90 days.[10]

Cryonics offers people the chance to freeze their body with the hope of coming back to life in the future. Corpses are embalmed with a glycerin-based solution, cooled under dry ice until they reach minus-202 degrees Fahrenheit, then gradually lowered into a pool of liquid nitrogen until the body reaches minus-320 degrees Fahrenheit. At that temperature, all movement of cells in the body have stopped. The goal of cryonics is that someday in the future, technology will come up with a way to clone or regenerate the preserved body.[11]

Promession is an environmentally-friendly way to dispose of human remains by freeze-drying. The body is frozen in liquid nitrogen to minus-320 degrees Fahrenheit, which crystallizes it. Percussive vibrations then pulverize the frozen body to disintegrate it into particles (think of how ice shatters), which are then freeze-dried, leaving approximately 30 percent of the original weight. Just like cremation, metals are separated from the freeze-dried remains either by magnetism or by sieving. The dry powder is placed in a biodegradable casket which is interred in the ground, and bacteria decompose what remains into humus in as little as six months to a year.[12]

State laws require the funeral home, cremation organization, or other person in charge of the deceased person's remains to prepare and file a death certificate. The certificate includes personal demographic information about the deceased (e.g., name, date of birth, address, cause of death, etc.) and is signed by a doctor, medical examiner, or coroner.[13] After the death certificate is filed, a burial permit will be issued. The permit identifies the disposition of remains chosen, and designates where the deceased will be buried, or the place and means where ashes will be scattered. Permits are required for all burials in the U.S.[14]

# SETTLING THE ESTATE

The old adage of death and taxes being the only certainties in life is true, but taxes arguably involve much less paperwork and duress. Just as you prepared your estate paperwork prior to your death, now your executor or beneficiaries set it all into action. When you're raw with emotion from a death is not the best time to battle with insurance companies and bureaucracies whose policies you are unfamiliar with. The countless details, arrangements, and planning can sometimes seem overwhelming and confusing because it comes at a time when people are not in the best place mentally to deal with it all. But just like the estate planning process, if sorting through the estate and settling matters is taken in small steps, it's not draining or difficult.

Most "few asset" estates with a will settle quickly. Complicated estates take longer, and if there's no will or trust, it can take years to get through probate. It absolutely cannot be emphasized enough: The better prepared your estate is before you die, generally the faster things will go settling your estate after your death. This will help your loved ones get past their grief much faster, rather than being emotionally drained for years fighting a bureaucracy—or other family members—over the estate.

After the funeral, or roughly a week to ten days after death, obtain death certificates so you can initiate settling the estate.

Generally, a certified copy of the death certificate will be needed to transfer ownership of each significant asset, such as cars, real estate, or bank accounts. Certified copies are also needed to claim life insurance policies, veterans' survivor benefits, and annuities. Certified copies are expensive, ranging from $20 to $40 each plus fees for certain forms of payment or processing. (On average, it generally requires ten death certificates to settle an estate.) To cut expenses when claiming benefits, ask if a non-certified photocopy is permitted, or if the company will return the original certified copy for reuse.[15] To obtain certified copies of a death certificate, contact your local Office of Vital Records (see Appendix A). If you used the services of a funeral home, they can also get copies on your behalf.

Next, contact the executor of the estate (for wills) or the trustee (for living trusts). If the deceased planned ahead, all of the necessary documents will be in a master file, and the executor or trustee can begin the process of settling the estate. The estate's executor can file for probate if necessary, as well as open a bank account for the estate. The executor may need to contact an accountant or tax preparer to see if an estate tax return or final income tax return should be filed; or a trust and estates attorney to assist with asset transfer and probate issues. (If you are not sure of something, or run into difficulty, seek legal assistance.)

Give all unpaid bills to the executor or trustee for payment. This includes utility bills, loans and mortgages, credit cards, rents, insurance, and property taxes. The executor can also ask companies to cancel the deceased's credit cards, and have final statements sent.

After the executor or trustee has been notified, contact government agencies, financial institutions, and insurers to start filing for benefits, or end current ones. This includes the deceased's investment adviser so you can obtain information on holdings; banks, to find accounts, activate payable-on-death (POD) accounts, and access safe deposit boxes; life insurers, to get claim forms; other insurance companies including property insurance, health and dental insurance; and long-term care insurance, so that policies can either be changed or canceled, and unused premiums can be returned to you.

Notify any insurance company with whom the deceased was insured. Ask for claim forms and instructions on how to file for life insurance proceeds. Many insurance companies will pay insurance proceeds into an interest-bearing account, giving the beneficiary time to make carefully considered decisions regarding the use of the money.[16]

Contact the administrator(s) of any IRA, 401(k) and/or 403(b) plans in which the deceased participated. These types of plans typically include a beneficiary designation to facilitate payment. If the deceased was receiving any pension benefits, contact the plan administrator. In some instances, the surviving spouse may be eligible to continue receiving all or part of the pension, either indefinitely or for a given period of time.

Contact Social Security and other agencies from which the deceased received benefits (such as Veterans Affairs) to either stop payments or ask about applicable survivor benefits. Be sure to contact any agencies that administer pension benefits or retirement plans, to either stop monthly checks or to get beneficiary claim forms. If the deceased served in the armed services, notify the Department of Veterans Affairs. A burial allowance may be available, subject to certain qualifications, and the spouse and minor children may be eligible for certain benefits. If the deceased was a union member, contact the union representative. Ask about any union benefits to which the deceased was entitled, as well as any benefits that may be available to the surviving spouse or minor children.[17]

If the death was job-related, contact your state's labor department for next steps, and to inquire about worker's compensation benefits. If the deceased owned a business, check with the state's revenue department to see if any business taxes are owed, or if estate tax is owed (generally only if the estate is worth more than $2 million). If the death was due to a criminal act, there may be benefits available from the state's crime victims compensation fund.

Call utility companies and other service providers to change or discontinue service. Some services like cable television, internet, and telephone can be canceled immediately, while it may be wise to delay others such as electric, water, gas, and lawn care so that the home can be properly maintained. It might be helpful to look over bank and credit card statements to identify other less obvious monthly recurring charges to cancel, like gym memberships, home security systems, and club membership dues. Also, ask the postal service to stop or forward mail.

If necessary, give notice of the death to the deceased's landlord and employer. Ask the employer about benefits, if there is any life insurance policy with the company, and any final pay due. Finally, notify the three major credit bureaus (Experian, Trans Union and Equifax) to prevent identity theft.

# CHAPTER EIGHT

# THE SCIENCE OF LOSS

Most people respond to a death by making a conscious effort to deal with the loss, while others will deny what happened to avoid it. Viewing the deceased body of a loved one can bring closure and mitigate grief. Dr. Erich Lindemann, a grief management pioneer, claims that a defining characteristic of people who struggle most with difficult or complicated grief are those who never saw the dead body of their loved one.[1] Acceptance of the loss increases as the shock of the realization that the person is really gone decreases. This can be why viewing the body is important, because at some deep level, we know what's true and can't deny it. In extreme cases, such as plane crashes, or crimes where the victim's remains are never recovered, survivors can be stubborn in their denial, and hold out false or unwarranted hope waiting for someone who isn't likely to return. This includes kidnap victims missing for years or decades, or a case such as missing Malaysian Air flight 370, which vanished over the southern Indian Ocean in March of 2014. The wreckage has never been found. "As long as there wasn't any evidence of a crash, of wounded or dead," said Ghyslain Wattrelos, a French businessman whose wife and two children were on the flight, "There was a little glimmer of hope."[2]

Grief can be easier to move through when it is due to a lingering death (like the majority of deaths), than with an accidental or violent death, which can cause survivors to feel excessively bereaved and anguished because they believe the person was taken "before their time." To quantify grief, pain, and loss in a general sense, the closer a person is to you, the greater the pain of the loss, which is then magnified by the manner of death. For example, the death of your own infant or child to an illness is going to feel way more intense than the loss of a distant relative or unrelated person, such as a neighbor. If your child is killed in a motor vehicle accident, the shock and pain are heightened. If your child is killed in a massive tragedy such as what occurred at Sandy Hook elementary school in Connecticut, the emotional trauma would literally be off the charts.

There is really no way to avoid experiencing pain caused by a loss, and unfortunately, death can bring out the worst in some people, because people tend to act out when they are in severe emotional pain. Often, long-standing family grievances (and some imaginary ones for sure), or family secrets, can be used as weapons on already distraught survivors as they fight over the deceased's estate. People will tell each other what they *really* think. Or worse, since no one likes to speak ill of the dead publicly, a false narrative of what the deceased was really like (which is nothing like what they were really like) is manufactured to keep peace. Some survivors use the sympathy they receive to manipulate and drain others of time, money, or emotions. ("I just lost my husband/or wife/or child, you can do this for me, can't you?")

Many people will seek out medication (or self-medication) in order to blunt or avoid the feelings of loss, which only prolongs the grief and pain. Drugs (legal or not) can't make the person come back. Ever. For a person who is emotionally distraught and feels lonely and abandoned, recovering from a loss may seem insurmountable, and may take months—or even years—to resolve. This is known as complicated grief, and mercifully, is not common. Grieving can also be made more difficult by lack of support from others, such as relatives who were estranged from the deceased. Also, if a survivor is unable to move on, and dwells on the loss, impatience for change may create a rift or increase tension between the bereaved and other members of the family.[3]

After lingering deaths, some people feel relieved that their deceased loved one is no longer suffering. Months of intense and draining caregiving can suddenly feel like a burden being lifted. People are not always severely anguished by a death. Research shows that most people can recover from loss on their own, over time, if they have social support and healthy habits. On average, it may take months or a year to come to terms with a loss, but contrary to popular (and unscientific) belief, there is no "normal" time period for someone to grieve.[4]

In the past decade, researchers possessing more advanced methods of data collection than their predecessors have uncovered major misconceptions about grief. Don't expect to pass through phases or stages of grief, since research indicates that most people do not go through a series of progressive steps that ultimately deposits them at a psychological finish line.[5] In reality, grief is a cluster of symptoms that come and go, until they eventually lift.[6] Studies also show that people who avoided facing their loss were no more depressed than people who worked through their grief. Also, research found that talking or writing about a death did not help people adjust to their loss any better than people who didn't.[7]

Researchers also identified specific patterns surrounding the intensity and duration of grief, and what they discovered is that the worst of grief is usually over within six months. Most people respond to loss with resilience—though loss may be forever, acute grief (thankfully) is not. A 2008 study of the results of more than 60 controlled studies on grief interventions found no evidence that counseling helped most bereaved individuals any more than the simple passage of time. Counseling may help a small minority of people, but it doesn't, on average, hasten grief's departure.[8] So most people are resilient enough to get through loss on their own, without stages, phases, or tasks. The old adage "time heals all wounds" seems truly viable in this regard.

After a death, support from family or caregivers is at its height for a little while, but eventually diminishes as people move on with life. The shock and pain wear off over time as normal activity is resumed, and the brain rewires itself from the trauma by overwriting those neuropathways to create new patterns. Eventually, survivors start rebuilding their lives, and direct energy into new activities and relationships.

# CHAPTER NINE

# NOTHING LASTS FOREVER

When you understand how death works, and most importantly, how much is actually in your power to prevent its hasty arrival, there's not much to fear. In fact, the physical mechanics of death are repetitive and almost boring: Everyone dies when the brain dies from lack of oxygen, whether it's caused by heart failure or by damage directly to the brain. So why would death be frightening? Is the scariness due to the unpredictability of when it will happen, and by what means? Or is it that you just can't imagine the world without you in it? Or both? By now it's obvious that it isn't due to death's physical mechanics alone.

What you think happens to a person's essence or personality at death (and after) depends on your religious and cultural beliefs. The prevailing understanding of conventional neuroscience is that human consciousness is something entirely dependent upon the billions-strong network of neurons in our brains, and as such, ceases to exist upon death.[1] While people can turn to philosophy, religion, and spirituality to create a comforting narrative that allows them to face death, it won't help anyone one bit in probate court. Taking pragmatic steps while alive, healthy, and not under duress is crucial to peace of mind when you die, because your loved ones will be secure, and will face the legal and financial path of least resistance in probate court (or during asset transfer if probate is bypassed). Think of it as a kind farewell gift.

If you're still apprehensive or fearful, remember these key points:

- Everyone knows they will die at some point. The fear comes from not knowing how and when, which then creates avoidance and denial.

- The more advance preparation you make for your own death, the more time your loved ones will have to spend with you to say goodbye at the end, instead of trying to make medical and financial decisions through the stress and haze of grief and loss. It's no coincidence that many clinicians have observed that the degree of family distress at the time of death is inversely related to the extent in which advance planning and preparation occurred.[2]

- It's better to have something legally documented, even if it needs to be corrected or amended later, than nothing at all.

- It costs a lot more to clean up a financial mess after a death than it does to prevent one by planning ahead.

- Estate planning documents aren't about how much money or how many things you have—they are about you having control over what happens to you and your family as you lay dying, and after you are gone. It's about your wishes being carried out. It's about you deciding who gets what you do have, regardless of the dollar value—and not a court making those decisions for you.

There is only one you, and the experience and memories of your life can never be replaced by anyone. No one else can have the same children, take the same vacations, or fall in love in exactly the same time, place, and circumstances that you did. No one can truly replace you—there really is no substitute for the original. Take the time, money, and effort to take care of yourself while you're alive. No one on their deathbed ever said, "Gee, I wish I'd worked another 40 hour week." You were not born to exist solely for the gratification of your place of employment—life is so much bigger than that. Don't fear death, but instead fear living a life where you could have done something—no matter how big or small—that mattered to you, or made life (or the world) better for those you leave behind, but didn't. Tell people how much you love them. You may never get to say goodbye should a sudden, instant death occur to you or someone close. Have your affairs in order, just in case.

Scientist Phil Plait has said that telling people there's no magic, afterlife, higher moral authoritarian father figure, security and "happily ever after" is a tough sell. It is, because from an evolutionary standpoint, our brains embrace faith and stories much easier than facts and data.[3] Know that it's far more satisfying to work and change things for the better while alive, instead of waiting for the imaginary perfection of an afterlife.

In the end, no matter how many people are by your bedside or not, we all die alone because none of those people are coming with us at that moment. And the more time elapses after our deaths, the more abstract we become to the living. Think about it: Does Abraham Lincoln evoke personal and emotional responses and familiar memories in you? Of course not. He's abstract because we didn't know him personally; we just know *of* him and admire his accomplishments. Even a monument of permanent recognition, such as having a street or a stadium named after us, won't stop us from fading in the public's mind and into abstraction after enough time has passed. Think of early 20th century New York mayor Fiorello LaGuardia, who had an airport named after him; or Jacob K. Javits, who was a New York politician for decades, and had a convention center named after him. You can't really think of them except abstractly, because you didn't know them, so you can't truly remember them. In a generation or two, we, too, will be completely forgotten, and thought of only in the abstract. Until we're eventually not remembered at all.

It can be painful to face the fact that life goes on without us. "One reason why death is terrifying is that it can mean that an individual will not be remembered by others," says social and behavioral health analyst Julie Framingham. "Death of the individual represents the obliteration of all the individual has worked for and aimed at for his or her entire life...The collective or social system will likely continue after the death of an individual member."[4] Neurologist Robert Burton wrote in his book,

*On Being Certain*: "Just before my mother died at age 97, I asked her what she had learned from her long life…In the hospital, her actual, penultimate words: 'In the end, I am only an ordinary person. No one special. No one to be remembered. Nothing.'"[5]

Nineteenth century English Romantic poet Percy Bysshe Shelley wrote a sonnet that explored the impermanence of people and their legacies, and the decay into oblivion of all things. But Shelley's sonnet *Ozymandias* isn't really a poem—it's the truth. About all of us.

# APPENDIX A: Checklists, Forms and Information

Links are listed by category in the general sequence in which they usually occur (pre-death and post-death). Links are not arranged by any particular preference or endorsement.

**Lawyers and State Bar Associations**
Find a qualified lawyer in your city:

- http://www.martindale.com
- http://www.avvo.com
- Also: lawguru.com, lawyers.com, legalmatch.com

State Bar Association contact information to find free legal clinics in your state:

- http://shop.americanbar.org/ebus/ABAGroups/DivisionforBarServices/BarAssociationDirectories/StateLocalBarAssociations.aspx

- http://www.lawyerlegion.com/promote-your-law-practice/directories-by-state-bar/
- http://legalpediaonline.wikidot.com/state-courts

## Wills – Explanations & Checklists

If you are going to write a will or have an attorney help you, use this checklist to speed up the process so you can arrive already prepared. The more prepared you are, the fewer expensive billable hours you'll incur:

- https://www.everplans.com/articles/checklist-writing-a-will
- https://www.everplans.com/articles/all-you-need-to-know-about-creating-a-will

## Trusts – Explanations & Checklists

Pros and cons of trusts (and their differences) explained:

- https://www.estateplanning.com/Understanding-Living-Trusts/
- https://quinnestatelaw.com/2013/02/revocable-versus-irrevocable-trusts/
- http://www.lifehealthpro.com/2013/08/09/revocable-vs-irrevocable-which-trust-is-right-for?page=2&slreturn=1485126411&page_all=1
- http://www.dummies.com/personal-finance/estate-planning/revocable-versus-irrevocable-trusts/
- http://irrevocable-trust.ultratrust.com/top-7-differences-between-irrevocable-trust-and-revocable-trust.html

- http://www.kaiserlawfirm.com/kaiserlaw/files/R evocableLivingTrustsBrochure09.pdf
- http://www.tn-elderlaw.com/resources/what-no-one-tells-you-about-living-trusts
- http://thismatter.com/money/wills-estates-trusts/
- http://thismatter.com/money/wills-estates-trusts/toc-trusts.htm
- Help for trustees under a revocable living trust (booklet explaining duties and responsibilities in detail) https://s3.amazonaws.com/files.consumerfinance .gov/f/201310_cfpb_lay_fiduciary_guides_trustee s.pdf

## Life Insurance

- How to claim a life insurance policy if you are the beneficiary: https://www.policygenius.com/blog/how-does-a-life-insurance-beneficiary-claim-a-policy/
- Types of life insurance: http://www.iii.org/article/what-are-different-types-term-life-insurance-policies
- Comparisons of insurance: https://www.farmers.com/life-insurance/coverage/term-life/value-term-life/
- Term vs. whole life comparison: https://www.matrixdirect.com/life-insurance-101/compare-product-options/term-vs-whole#fv

\* \* \*

NOTE: In most cases, the following documents must be witnessed by two people who are not related to you, and notarized, in order to be legally binding. Check the laws for your state to see what's required. Free notary public services can usually be found at banks and credit unions; city or county government offices such as county clerks and court houses; title companies; public libraries; college campuses if you are as student; military bases or offices; hotels; concierges; insurance companies, and public legal services.

## Estate Planning Checklists, Legal Documents, and Forms

This includes wills, power of attorney forms, living trusts, etc. Some online coupon websites like groupon.com or retailmenot.com will have discount codes for some of the paid online legal services listed below.

- Basic explanation of what an estate plan is and does: https://www.rocketlawyer.com/estate-planning-guide/what-is-an-estate.rl
- Digital estate planning laws for each state: https://www.everplans.com/articles/state-by-state-digital-estate-planning-laws
- Estate planning basics: http://law.freeadvice.com/estate_planning/estate_planning/
- Estate planning checklists: https://www.everplans.com/checklists
- Another estate planning checklist: http://thismatter.com/money/wills-estates-trusts/estate-planning-checklist.htm

- Free, simple questionnaire that determines what legal documents you need for your specific situation: https://www.legalzoom.com/personal/estate-planning/help-me-decide.html#/questions-1
- Free online forms for wills, trusts, DPOAs, health care and amendments/codicils: http://www.lawdepot.com/contracts/groups/estate/
- Free advance directive forms, digital estate laws, organ donation registries, probate forms and more: https://www.everplans.com/guides/state-by-state-guides
- Free estate planning documents: https://www.rocketlawyer.com/estate-planning.rl
- Different types of power of attorney explained: http://legalbeagle.com/5366625-power-vs-durable-power-attorney.html
- http://estate.findlaw.com/living-will/the-definition-of-power-of-attorney-living-will-and-advance.html
- Free customized estate and health care forms you can complete in ten minutes or less: http://www.lawdepot.com/contracts/groups/estate/
- Free POA form generator; explains each type very well: https://legaltemplates.net/form/power-of-attorney/
- Free state-by-state advance directives forms: http://www.imsorrytohear.com/resources/advance-directives and http://www.aarp.org/home-

family/caregiving/free-printable-advance-directives/

- Free or low-cost durable power of attorney for financial forms for all 50 states: http://powerofattorney.com/durable/

- Living wills, POA, DNR guide: http://www.caringinfo.org/i4a/pages/index.cfm?pageid=1

- Advanced care planning: http://www.caringinfo.org/files/public/brochures/End-of-Life_Decisions.pdf

- Free "Notice of Revocation" forms to cancel a power of attorney: https://www.lawdepot.com/contracts/revocation-of-power-of-attorney/ and https://www.rocketlawyer.com/document/revocation-of-power-of-attorney.rl#/

- Comparison of the most popular online legal services (RocketLawyer, LegalZoom and Willing): http://www.gyst.com/articles/the-gyst-review-of-diy-digital-wills

- Another online legal planning services site: https://www.policygenius.com/blog/willing-review-should-you-write-your-will-online/

- Create a legally binding will online in ten minutes for free: https://willing.com/

- Complete, low-cost, one-stop-shopping estate planning service, storage, funeral wishes, organ donation and legal review: https://www.uslegalwills.com/howdoesitwork

- Free online will at RocketLawyer:

https://www.rocketlawyer.com/form/last-will-and-testament.rl#/

- Online will (with optional bundle of other services including attorney advice) with prices starting at $69: https://www.legalzoom.com/personal/estate-planning/last-will-and-testament-overview.html

- Expatriate wills for assets in Canada, the U.K., and the U.S.: https://www.uslegalwills.com/Prices

- Ask a free legal question online: http://www.avvo.com

- Fifteen minutes of legal advice for $39: https://www.avvo.com/advisor

- Low-cost legal forms only: http://www.smartlegalforms.com/

- All-in-one, one-stop-shopping for wills, DPOAs, trusts, etc. stored online for $75/year (but has a free 30-day trial): https://www.everplans.com/pricing

- The ease of PODs: http://www.nolo.com/legal-encyclopedia/question-set-up-payable-on-death-account-28260.html

- Online legal articles: http://www.nolo.com/legal-encyclopedia

## Disposition Authorization of Remains Forms

These legal documents allow you to specify how you want your remains handled (i.e., burial, cremation, etc.). Search online for your state's requirements and forms; below are Washington and Wisconsin examples.

- http://endoflifewa.org/wp-content/uploads/2015/01/Disposition-Authorization.pdf
- https://www.dhs.wisconsin.gov/forms/f0/f00086.pdf

## Body and Organ Donation Programs
- Whole body donation programs for science and research by state: http://anatbd.acb.med.ufl.edu/usprograms/
- Sign up for organ donation online: https://organize.org/ and https://www.organdonor.gov/register.html

## POLST (Physician's Orders for Life-Sustaining Treatment) Forms
- What is a POLST form?: https://www.everplans.com/articles/whats-a-polst-physicians-orders-for-life-sustaining-treatment
- Free POLST forms for each state: https://www.everplans.com/articles/state-by-state-polst-forms

## End-of-life Stages
Signs of impending death:
- https://palliative.stanford.edu/transition-to-death/signs-of-impending-death/
- http://www.palliativecarensw.org.au/pdfs/PCNSW-Signs-Symptoms-of-Approaching-Death-ARTICLE.pdf

## Checklists of Immediate Steps to Take After Death

- http://www.legalvoice.org/after-death-occurs-checklist
- http://diesmart.com/sayinggoodbye/immediately-after-death/
- http://www.consumerreports.org/cro/magazine/2012/10/what-to-do-when-a-loved-one-dies/index.htm

## Funeral planning checklists

- State-by-state list of your funeral planning rights: http://www.imsorrytohear.com/resources/state-by-state-end-of-life-guides
- Excellent tutorial site explaining what is needed and why: http://diesmart.com/estate-planning/
- How to choose a funeral home, set a budget, and shop around: https://www.funerals.org/consumers/
- Funeral Plans Checklist: See PDF pages 5-11: http://www.dow.com/friends/pdfs/Full_Funeral_Planning_Guide.pdf
- Planning: https://www.funerals.org/consumers/?consumers=four-step-funeral-planning
- Checklist: https://www.funeral-burial-insurance.com/Funeral-Planning-Checklist.pdf
- Checklist and forms: http://www.imsorrytohear.com/uploads/PDFs/ISTH%20Funeral%20Planning%20Checklist%20and%20Forms.pdf

- Planning: http://funeralconsume.wpengine.com/product/go-funeral-planner-spiral-bound-includes-state-chapter-final-rights/
- Checklist: http://www.sharedsorrows.com/plan-a-funeral/post-funeral-checklist/
- Checklist: http://www.sharedsorrows.com/plan-a-funeral/time-of-loss-checklist/
- A to Z funeral encyclopedia http://www.imsorrytohear.com/resources
- Funeral costs: https://www.parting.com/blog/how-much-does-the-average-funeral-cost/
- Funeral expense calculators and worksheets: http://www.sharedsorrows.com/funerals-for-less/
- Inexpensive cremation services (shows prices) by state: http://www.dfsmemorials.com/usa.php
- Direct cremation prices and providers in your area: http://www.us-funerals.com/funeral-articles/finding-a-low-cost-cremation-provider.html
- Funeral shipping when someone dies out of state or country: http://www.us-funerals.com/funeral-articles/when-death-occurs-away-from-home.html
- Funeral planning checklist: https://www.funeral-burial-insurance.com/Funeral-Planning-Checklist.pdf
- Federal Trade Commission booklet titled Shopping for Funeral Services: https://www.consumer.ftc.gov/articles/pdf-0056-funerals.pdf and website:

https://www.consumer.ftc.gov/articles/0070-shopping-funeral-services

## Funeral Assistance Programs
- Funeral financial assistance programs by state: http://www.imsorrytohear.com/blog/funeral-assistance-for-those-who-need-it/
- Excellent guide about what to do if you can't afford a funeral: http://www.imsorrytohear.com/blog/paying-for-a-funeral-what-do-i-do-if-i-cant-afford-a-funeral/
- Low-income funeral programs: http://dfsmemorials.com/cremation-blog/funeral-burial-resources-low-income-uninsured-families/

## Obtaining Death Certificates
- State-by-state contact guide for obtaining death certificates: https://www.cdc.gov/nchs/w2w/index.htm
- Death certificate info needed: See PDF page 4 (http://www.dow.com/friends/pdfs/Full_Funeral_Planning_Guide.pdf)

## Probate
- Easiest guide to understanding probate: https://www.everplans.com/articles/how-to-understand-probate-court
- State-by-state probate laws: https://www.everplans.com/articles/state-by-state-probate-laws

- Why avoid probate?: http://www.nolo.com/legal-encyclopedia/why-avoid-probate-29861.html
- How to avoid probate with estate planning methods: http://www.nolo.com/legal-encyclopedia/avoid-probate-how-to-30235.html
- State-by-state rules to avoid probate: http://www.nolo.com/legal-encyclopedia/avoiding-probate-in-your-state-31015.html

## Small Estates

- American Bar Association synopsis of small estate requirements for all 50 states: http://www.americanbar.org/publications/probate_property_magazine_2012/2014/july_august_2014/2014_aba_rpte_pp_v28_4_article_blumberg_51_flavors_survey_of_small_estate_procedures.html
- Small estate laws for all 50 states: http://www.nolo.com/legal-encyclopedia/probate-shortcuts-in-your-state-31020.html
- Small estate affidavit forms for each state, and then each county: http://smallestateaffidavit.com/free-small-estate-affidavit-form/
- Free small estate affidavit forms for each state: https://formswift.com/affidavit-of-small-estate
- You can also enter the state you live in and the term "small estate affidavit form" in your preferred online search engine. State government

agencies often have these forms available to download for free.

## Social Security

- How to report a death to Social Security: http://thelawdictionary.org/article/how-to-report-a-death-to-social-security/
- How much survivors can expect to receive: https://www.ssa.gov/planners/survivors/onyour own5.html
- How to apply for Social Security benefits after a death in the family: https://www.ssa.gov/planners/survivors/howtoa pply.html
- Social Security survivors benefits guide: https://www.ssa.gov/pubs/EN-05-10084.pdf
- How Social Security can help when a family member dies: https://www.ssa.gov/pubs/EN-05-10008.pdf

## Taxes

- How to get a taxpayer ID for an estate: https://www.irs.gov/pub/irs-pdf/fss4.pdf. For help filling out the form: http://thelawdictionary.org/article/how-to-obtain-a-tax-id-number-for-an-estate/
- How to file a deceased person's tax return: https://www.irs.gov/uac/how-do-i-file-a-deceased-persons-tax-return and https://www.irs.gov/businesses/small-businesses-

self-employed/deceased-taxpayers-filing-the-final-returns-of-a-deceased-taxpayer

## Digital/Online Cloud Storage

These are services that will store copies of your documents, which protects against theft, fire, flood, or other natural disasters. They can be accessed anywhere, from any device.

- Store and share your documents choices guide: https://www.gyst.com/articles/store-a-will-living-will-and-advance-directives
- MedicAlert: https://www.medicalert.org/dnr/types-of-documents-to-store
- U.S. Living Will Registry: http://www.uslivingwillregistry.com/

Free cloud-based file storage and sharing:
- List of the top eight free file storage sites to compare: http://www.adweek.com/digital/top-15-free-online-file-storage-sites-2/
- Google Drive (http://drive.google.com). Use your Gmail account login to sign in.
- Dropbox: https://www.dropbox.com/?landing=fd
- Box: https://www.box.com/

Subscription-based secure/encrypted online storage:
- CertainSafe: https://certainsafe.com/
- Carbonite: https://www.carbonite.com/

## Password Managers

For computer and digital accounts, make a list of usernames and passwords and store them in your master document file. Free online services (i.e., LastPass) make this task very easy, so you can just print out the contents of your password vault and keep it in your master file.

- Compare password manager services: http://www.techradar.com/news/software/applic ations/the-best-password-manager-1325845
- LastPass: https://www.lastpass.com/
- Dashlane: https://www.dashlane.com/
- 1Password: https://1password.com/

## Miscellaneous

- Military burial at sea http://www.navy.mil/navydata/nav_legacy.asp? id=204
- Burial at sea, non-military: https://www.epa.gov/ocean-dumping/burial-sea#instructions
- Executor's guide: https://store.nolo.com/products/the-executors-guide-exec.html and https://www.amazon.com/Executors-Guide-Settling-Loved-Estate/dp/1413322298
- Online forum for death discussion: http://www.deathub.com/
- Free Excel spreadsheet checklist of estate planning info to compile for your survivors: https://s3.amazonaws.com/static-gyst-com/content/My_GYST_Digital_Details.xlsx

## CDC Data

CDC's WISQARS™ (Web-based Injury Statistics Query and Reporting System) is an interactive, online database that provides fatal and nonfatal injury, violent death, and cost of injury data from a variety of trusted sources.

- Data and statistics:
  https://www.cdc.gov/injury/wisqars/facts.html
- Mortality data:
  https://www.cdc.gov/nchs/nvss/mortality_related.htm

# APPENDIX B:
# Documents To-Do Checklist

The documents listed below are the legal means to carry out your specific wishes as you near death, and afterward. Keep things simple by crossing off what you don't need or what isn't applicable to you. Then, pick an item and work on it for 15 minutes a day until it's complete. Use the detailed checklists and free or low-cost resources in Appendix A to help you complete each step. When you're all done, see Appendix C for information on how to store all the documents securely.

Create the following documents that best suit your needs. Always list one or two alternates in case the person you prefer to act on your behalf is unable to, or precedes you in death. Don't hesitate to ask an attorney for advice.

_____ Will

_____ Codicil to existing will (if needed)

_____ Living Trust

_____ Amendments to living trust (if needed)

_____ Guardianship/Custody of children (usually written into will)

_____ Disposition authorization form (instructions for your remains)

_____ Final arrangements letter (instructions for funeral ceremony
       details)

_____ Living will/Advanced care directive

_____ Durable power of attorney: Medical

_____ Durable power of attorney: Financial

_____ Durable power of attorney: Digital

_____ Pet Trust/Guardianship with instructions for care and financial
       support

_____ Residual will with beneficiary and general instructions

_____ Obtain and complete POD and TOD forms

_____ Obtain blank Small Estate Affidavit forms to keep on file for
       survivors (if applicable)

_____ Purchase life insurance

_____ List of digital assets with logon and password info

# APPENDIX C:
# Master Document File

The most efficient and effective way to store all documents, contacts, contracts, and other relevant information is in one master file. You can create a binder, a folder, or digitize everything needed onto an encrypted USB drive. Then, store your file in a safe and secure place, and let your family and future executor know where to find it. Personal safes cost between $100-$500, but you can also store the file in a lockbox with a storage lock (it uses a key rather than a combination) to seal it for $25 or less. If you want to scan and store it all digitally, you could store it in an encrypted or password-protected online cloud service (See Appendix A), or use an encrypted USB drive, and store the drive in a safe place.

The information to be stored can be sorted by the following categories in your file to make it easier for your survivors to quickly locate:

1) Important Contacts

2) Personal Information

3) Legal Documents

4) Medical Documents

5) Financial Accounts: a) assets and b) liabilities

6) Other/Miscellaneous

Store the original documents from Appendix B in the master file to keep key personal, medical, and financial information accessible. Don't store documents in a safe deposit box, because many of the documents—such as healthcare and financial proxies—will need to be accessed before your death, and most wills aren't filed and read until *after* a funeral. If you absolutely *must* store your documents in a safe deposit box, make sure that someone close to you has a key to the box, or knows where to find one. Copies of wills, powers of attorney, advance medical directives, etc., can be kept with an attorney, or in another safe but accessible place.

To save time from having to write out all of the names, addresses, and phone numbers of professional advisers such as bankers, attorneys, stockbrokers, and insurance agents, you can attach the contact person or company's business card to original documents or monthly statements. Also include your most recent statements that have identifying information such as the company or vendor name (i.e., Verizon), your account number, and a company contact phone number.

If a section or item below doesn't apply to you, cross it off and put "N/A" for not applicable next to it so that your survivors don't think that something is missing.

Each year on a holiday you can remember (such as Memorial Day), review and update your master document file. Also, confirm each year that your family members and future executor know where to locate it.

## 1) IMPORTANT CONTACTS

| | Company or Firm Name | Contact Person | Phone Number |
|---|---|---|---|
| **Executor (will) or Trustee (trust)** | | | |
| **Lawyer** | | | |
| **Accountant** | | | |
| **Financial Adviser** | | | |
| **Insurance Agent** | | | |
| **Stockbroker** | | | |
| **Banker (w/branch address)** | | | |
| **Employer** | | | |
| **Landlord** | | | |
| **Doctor (general practitioner)** | | | |
| **Doctor (specialist)** | | | |
| **Dentist** | | | |
| **Other** | | | |

## 2) PERSONAL INFORMATION – Photocopy or originals for each

- Social Security card (or number)
- Birth certificates (for all family members)
- Marriage license or certificate
- Court documents for name changes
- Passport
- Green card number, citizenship, immigration and/or alien registration papers
- Domestic partnership registration
- Court documents for adoptions
- Court documents for divorce (including settlement agreements and prenuptial agreements)
- Community Property agreements
- Armed Forces/Military records, including discharge papers
- Union affiliation (name and contact info)

## 3) LEGAL DOCUMENTS – Photocopy or originals for each

### Will

- Copy of current will and any codicils
- Copy of previous versions of the will
- Attorney or law firm that created the will, or name and URL of online legal service

### Trusts

- Declarations of trust or trust agreements and any amendments

- Attorney or law firm that created the trust, or name and URL of online legal service
- Bank accounts associated with the trust (name and branch location)

### Other Legal Documents
- Durable Power of Attorney: Medical
- Durable Power of Attorney: Financial
  Durable Power of Attorney: Digital
- Living Will/Advanced Care Directive
- Disposition Authorization
- Pre-paid funeral contracts

## 4) MEDICAL DOCUMENTS

Make photocopies of all wallet insurance cards, and store originals of the most recent premium payments.

Organ/tissue donation record
Automatically Renewing Medications
- Names of medications
- Name of pharmacy where medications are renewed
- Name of doctor who prescribed medications
- Medical Insurance – Coverage type (e.g., group, individual, Medicare, Medicare Supplement, Medicaid)

>       Plan ID#:
>       Group ID #:
>       Contact Name:
>       Telephone:

- Dental Insurance – Include premium payment records
                Plan ID#:
                Group ID #:
                Contact Name:
                Telephone:

Long-term care insurance
Private health insurance
Workers' Compensation

## 5) FINANCIAL ACCOUNTS – ASSETS

Use a copy of the most recent statements for all accounts. List the beneficiaries for each (where applicable) if they aren't shown on the documents.

### Income Sources
Businesses owned
Income statements for the current year (Social Security, pension, IRA's, annuities, employment, and other income records)
Disability payment documents (State, Veterans, etc.)

### Banking
Safe deposit box location and authorized users
Safe deposit box keys location
Savings account – Account number and branch location
Checking account – Account number and branch location
Money Market – Account number and branch location

ATM/Debit Card – Account number and branch location
Certificate of Deposit – Maturity date
Copies of PODs or TODs
Logon and password for online banking

**Investments & Pensions**
Brokerage account #1
Brokerage account #2
Stocks and bonds
Mutual fund accounts
Investment portfolios
IRA
Roth IRA

Simplified Employee Pension (SEP) plan
Plan Administrator – Contact name and phone number

Salary Reduction Simplified Employee Pension (SARSEP) plan
Plan Administrator – Contact name and phone number

Company Pension – Company name and account number
Plan Administrator – Contact name and phone number

Company Pension – Company name and account number
Plan Administrator – Contact name and phone number

Union Pension
Union name & Local #
Plan Administrator – Contact name and phone number

401(k) / 403(b) Plan
Plan Administrator – Contact name and phone number

401(k) / 403(b) Plan
Plan Administrator – Contact name and phone number

## **Property – Include copies or originals of deeds and titles**

Real Estate – Property  No. 1
Real Estate – Property  No. 2
Real Estate – Property  No. 3
Business Property No. 1
Business Property No. 2
Car No. 1
Car No. 2
Car No. 3
Boat
RV
Motorcycle
Artwork
Jewelry
Collections
Other
Other

## **Insurance Policies – Include premium payment records**

Life
Annuity
Accidental Death &  Dismemberment

Disability
Homeowners
Renters
Car No. 1
Car No. 2
Car No. 3
Other Insurance
Other Insurance

## FINANCIAL ACCOUNTS – LIABILITIES

### Taxes
IRS income tax returns (for the current and previous year)
IRS gift tax returns (for all years)
State income tax records and returns
Property tax records and statements

### Loans
1st Mortgage
2nd Mortgage
Home Equity Line of Credit
Reverse Mortgage
Personal loans
Student loans
Auto
Auto
Boat
RV
Motorcycle

Other

Other

## Credit Cards

Photocopy the front of credit cards and store them with copies of the most recent statement(s) showing the account number and contact phone of the card issuer.

## 6) OTHER/MISCELLANEOUS

### Utility Bills

Electric

Gas

Heating

Water/Sewer

Garbage

Phone

Cable TV

Internet

### Club Memberships

Sports clubs (i.e., golf or country club)

Health and fitness clubs

Discount warehouse merchants (i.e., Costco)

### Digital Assets and Accounts

Internet service provider name and account number or copy of last statement

**List of Usernames and Passwords to Log on To:**
Desktop computer 1
Desktop computer 2
Laptop computer 1
Laptop computer 2
Tablet 1
Tablet 2
Cellphone 1 (Copy of monthly statement or service plan)
Cellphone 2 (Copy of monthly statement or service plan)

**Email Accounts**
Gmail
Yahoo! Mail
Other

**Online Merchants**
Amazon
Ebay
Other
Other

**Social Media**
Facebook
Twitter
LinkedIn
Pinterest
Instagram
Snapchat
Other

**<u>Miscellaneous Online Accounts</u>**

Cloud storage

Movies and TV: (iTunes, Netflix, Hulu)

Photos: (Picasa, Shutterfly)

Books and audiobooks: (Amazon, Barnes & Noble, Kindle)

Newspaper websites: (New York Times, Washington Post)

Music: (Pandora, Spotify)

Gaming

Coupons or discounts (Groupon, Retail me not)

Airline miles

Travel: (Orbitz, Priceline)

Digital money: (PayPal, Bitcoin)

Art or creative products: (eBooks, podcasts, etsy, Craigslist, eBay)

Domain names or websites:

Intellectual property: (copyrights, trademarks, patents)

Storing and sharing: (Dropbox, SecureDrop)

Crowdsourcing (GoFundMe, Kickstarter)


### * * * FILE ALL OF THE ABOVE IN YOUR MASTER DOCUMENT FILE * * *

# ENDNOTES

## INTRODUCTION

1 *Breaking Bad*, created by Vince Gilligan. Episode 8 "Hermanos" from Season 4 originally aired on AMC in the United States on September 4, 2011.

## CHAPTER 1 – FACING OBLIVION

1 http://www.endoflife.northwestern.edu/last_hours_of_living/module12.pdf

2 http://usatoday30.usatoday.com/news/health/2005-10-04-death-timeline_x.htm

3 http://www.apa.org/pi/aging/programs/eol/end-of-life-factsheet.pdf American Psychological Association citing Foley, 1995; Isaacs & Knickman, 1997.

4 Jennie Dear. "What It Feels Like to Die. Science is just beginning to understand the experience of life's end." *The Atlantic*, SEP 9, 2016. http://www.theatlantic.com/health/archive/2016/09/what-it-feels-like-to-die/499319/?

utm_source=nl-atlantic-weekly-091616

5    http://www.calebwilde.com/2014/10/my-tedx-talk-embracing-death/

## CHAPTER 2 – CONTROL

1    Framingham, Julie, and Martell L. Teasley. *Behavioral Health Response to Disasters*. Boca Raton: CRC Press, 2012. Section 6.2.3.5 Effects and Changes in Personal Worldview and Assumptions and 6.5.2.3 Bolstering Culturally Constructed Self-Esteem

2    https://www.epa.gov/sites/production/files/2015-09/documents/webpopulationrsuperfundsites9.28.15.pdf

3    https://www.ncbi.nlm.nih.gov/pubmed/26675728

4    http://jamanetwork.com/journals/jamaoncology/article-abstract/2522371 and http://prostate.net/articles/preventing-cancer-isnt-rocket-science

5    http://go.nature.com/2kjbRHN and http://prostate.net/articles/preventing-cancer-isnt-rocket-science

6    https://www.cdc.gov/physicalactivity/basics/adults/ and http://www.who.int/dietphysicalactivity/factsheet_adults/en/

7    https://www.cancer.gov/about-cancer/causes-prevention/risk/alcohol/alcohol-fact-sheet and http://onlinelibrary.wiley.com/doi/10.1111/add.13477/full and http://www.medscape.com/viewarticle/824237

8    http://onlinelibrary.wiley.com/doi/10.1111/add.13477/full

9    http://media.jamanetwork.com/news-item/pictures-warning-of-smoking-dangers-on-cigarette-packs-increased-quit-attempts/ and https://www.sciencedaily.com/releases/2016/06/160606115532.htm. The Food and Drug Administration had proposed nine graphic warning labels in June 2011, which had faced opposition from tobacco companies since, spurring legal battles. Four of the five largest U.S. tobacco companies sued the federal government Aug. 16, 2011, over the new graphic cigarette labels, saying the warnings violate their free speech rights and will cost millions of dollars to print. http://www.cbsnews.com/news/fdas-graphic-cigarette-labels-rule-goes-up-in-smoke-after-us-abandons-appeal/

Despite their effectiveness in other countries such as Canada and the UK, tobacco industry litigation stalled a 2011 proposal to add such warnings to U.S. cigarette packs, the study authors noted. In

2012, the U.S. Circuit Court of Appeals for the District of Columbia found that the U.S. Food and Drug Administration's proposed rule violated tobacco companies' First Amendment commercial speech rights. More than 70 countries have adopted or are considering such warnings. Pictorial warning labels have had a significant impact on smoking rates in the studied countries, the investigators found. Eight years after Canada implemented the warnings, smoking prevalence fell by 12 to 20 percent compared to the period before those warnings were in effect. In the United Kingdom, smoking declined 10 percent the year after the warnings were introduced.
http://www.upi.com/Health_News/2016/11/03/Graphic-images-on-cigarette-packs-may-cut-US-smoking-deaths/4991478223808/

10   You can find some of them here: http://www.theguardian.pe.ca/content/dam/tc/the-guardian/images/2011/9/27/09272011-1861987.jpg and here http://www.nytimes.com/2011/06/22/health/policy/22smoke.html and here: http://media.jamanetwork.com/wp-content/uploads/2016/06/pictorialwarningscroppedfigureFINAL-vert.jpg. For info on the lawsuit, see: http://www.cbsnews.com/ news/fdas-graphic-cigarette-labels-rule-goes-up-in-smoke-after-us-abandons-appeal/

11   http://www.lung.org/stop-smoking/i-want-to-quit/how-to-quit-smoking.html?referrer=https://www.google.com/ and https://smokefree.gov/

12   http://www.diabetes.org/diabetes-basics/genetics-of-diabetes.html?referrer=https://www.google.com/

13   https://www.nytimes.com/2016/04/22/health/us-suicide-rate-surges-to-a-30-year-high.html?_r=0

14   https://www.cdc.gov/nchs/products/databriefs/db241.htm

15   http://www.biography.com/people/jack-kevorkian-9364141#synopsis

16   http://www.medscape.com/viewarticle/742070_3

17   https://en.wikipedia.org/wiki/Legality_of_euthanasia

18   https://en.wikipedia.org/wiki/Jack_Kevorkian

19   http://www.snohomishcountywa.gov/ArchiveCenter/ViewFile/Item/4229 page 23.

20  http://www.gallup.com/poll/193082/euthanasia-acceptable-solid-majority.aspx

21  http://harpers.org/archive/2016/01/when-i-die/

22  http://www.medscape.com/viewarticle/742070_3

23  https://www.deathwithdignity.org/faqs/

24  http://www.medscape.com/viewarticle/742070_3

25  https://www.deathwithdignity.org/faqs/

26  https://en.wikipedia.org/wiki/Secobarbital and http://www.npr.org/ sections/health-shots/2016/03/23/471595323/ drug-company-jacks-up-cost-of-aid-in-dying-medication

27  https://www.deathwithdignity.org/faqs/

28  http://mynorthwest.com/521630/seattle-program-helps-comfort-homeless-people-in-their-final-days/

29  http://mynorthwest.com/521630/seattle-program-helps-comfort-homeless-people-in-their-final-days/

## CHAPTER 3 – PLANNING & PREPARING

1  http://thismatter.com/money/wills-estates-trusts/overview-intestacy-wills-trusts-estates-probate.htm

2  http://estate.findlaw.com/planning-an-estate/understanding-intestacy-if-you-die-without-an-estate-plan.html

3  http://legal-dictionary.thefreedictionary.com/probate

4  http://thelawdictionary.org/article/how-to-probate-a-will/

5  http://www.osbar.org/public/legalinfo/1117_probate.htm

6  http://www.nolo.com/legal-encyclopedia/why-avoid-probate-29861.html

7  http://www.kaiserlawfirm.com/kaiserlaw/files/RevocableLiving TrustsBrochure09.pdf

8  http://law.freeadvice.com/estate_planning/probate/is_no_will.htm

9  http://info.legalzoom.com/entitled-vehicle-after-person-dies-not-included-trust-21602.html

10  http://www.tn-elderlaw.com/resources/what-no-one-tells-you-about-living-trusts

11  http://smallestateaffidavit.com/

12  http://endoflife.northwestern.edu/last_hours_of_living/part_on e.pdf

13  https://www.debt.com/2016/will-power-will-important-people-dont-one/

14  https://www.debt.com/2016/will-power-will-important-people-dont-one/

15  https://www.debt.com/2016/will-power-will-important-people-dont-one/

16  http://www.usatoday.com/story/money/personalfinance/2015/07/11/estate-plan-will/71270548/

17  http://www.city-data.com/forum/retirement/1428127-why-dont-people-write-wills.html

18  https://www.uslegalwills.com/blog/notorious-wills-of-the-rich-and-famous/#more-1830

19  http://www.vulture.com/2016/08/prince-estate-will-chaos.html

20  http://time.com/money/4308204/prince-dies-without-will/

21  http://time.com/money/4308204/prince-dies-without-will/

22  http://www.hollywoodreporter.com/thr-esq/princes-legal-legacy-contract-fights-886521

23  http://www.chicagotribune.com/entertainment/music/ct-prince-estate-20160427-story.html

24  http://www.billboard.com/articles/news/7408814/prince-executives-retained-estate-management

25  http://www.pricelawpractice.com/posts/why-princes-lack-of-a-will-is-a-lesson-to-everyone-on-estate-planning/ and http://www.vulture.com/2016/08/prince-estate-will-chaos.html

26  http://www.city-data.com/forum/retirement/1428127-why-dont-people-write-wills.html

## CHAPTER 4 – WHAT YOU NEED FOR WHAT YOU HAVE

1  https://www.legalzoom.com/personal/estate-planning/compare.html

2  https://www.estateplanning.com/Understanding-Living-Trusts/

3  http://estate.findlaw.com/living-will/the-definition-of-power-of-attorney-living-will-and-advance.html

4 https://www.debt.com/2016/will-power-will-important-people-dont-one/

5 http://www.americanbar.org/content/newsletter/publications/gp_solo_magazine_home/gp_solo_magazine_index/petestateplanning.html and http://www.aspca.org/pet-care/pet-planning/pet-trust-primer

6 http://blogs.findlaw.com/law_and_life/2014/04/should-you-include-burial-plans-in-your-will.html

7 http://blogs.findlaw.com/law_and_life/2014/04/should-you-include-burial-plans-in-your-will.html

8 https://www.thebalance.com/revocable-vs-irrevocable-trusts-3505386

9 http://www.nolo.com/legal-encyclopedia/avoid-probate-how-to-30235.html

10 https://www.legalzoom.com/articles/top-three-benefits-of-a-living-trust

11 https://www.estateplanning.com/Understanding-Living-Trusts/

12 https://www.thebalance.com/what-does-the-michael-jackson-family-trust-say-3505325 and https://www.thebalance.com/what-does-michael-jackson-s-will-say-3505324 and http://hosted.ap.org/specials/interactives/_documents/jackson_will.pdf

13 https://www.thebalance.com/what-does-the-michael-jackson-family-trust-say-3505325 and https://www.thebalance.com/what-does-michael-jackson-s-will-say-3505324 and http://hosted.ap.org/specials/interactives/_documents/jackson_will.pdf

14 https://www.thebalance.com/how-to-keep-your-estate-plan-private-3505375

15 Molly Edmonds. "How Dying Works" 12 January 2009. HowStuffWorks.com. <http://health.howstuffworks.com/diseases-conditions/death-dying/dying.htm>

16 http://www.nolo.com/legal-encyclopedia/question-what-power-of-attorney-what-28327.html

17 http://estate.findlaw.com/living-will/the-definition-of-power-of-attorney-living-will-and-advance.html

18   https://www.rocketlawyer.com/estate-planning-guide/living-will-vs-power-of-attorney.rl

19   http://www.nolo.com/legal-encyclopedia/question-what-power-of-attorney-what-28327.html

20   https://en.wikipedia.org/wiki/Terri_Schiavo_case

21   http://www.nbcnews.com/id/8225637/ns/us_news/t/schiavo-autopsyshows-irreversiblebrain-damage/?hasFlash=true&

22   https://www.estateplanning.com/Understanding-Living-Trusts/

23   http://estate.findlaw.com/living-will/the-definition-of-power-of-attorney-living-will-and-advance.html and
     http://www.brighamandwomensfaulkner.org/about-us/patient-visitor-information/advance-care-directives/dnr-orders.aspx

24   http://www.polst.org/wp-content/uploads/2015/01/2013.09.26-Final-POLST-Article.pdf and http://polst.org/advance-care-planning/polst-and-advance-directives/

25   http://www.washingtonlawhelp.org/files/C9D2EA3F-0350-D9AF-ACAE-BF37E9BC9FFA/attachments/392A5117-D581-FCE9-5EF2-E382E46B92AC/9608en_power-of-attorney-2016.pdf

26   http://www.sweeneyprobatelaw.com/Articles/PAYABLE-ON-DEATH -POD-AND-TRANSFER-ON-DEATH-TOD-ACCOUNTS. shtml

27   http://www.nolo.com/legal-encyclopedia/naming-tod-beneficiary.html

28   https://www.nolo.com/legal-encyclopedia/free-books/avoid-probate-book/chapter5-3.html

29   https://www.irs.gov/help-resources/tools-faqs/faqs-for-individuals/ frequently-asked-tax-questions-answers/interest-dividends-other-types-of-income/life-insurance-disability-insurance-proceeds/life-insurance-disability-insurance-proceeds

30   http://www.pbs.org/pov/homegoings/economics-of-the-funeral-industry/

31   http://www.pbs.org/pov/homegoings/economics-of-the-funeral-industry/

32   http://www.aarp.org/money/scams-fraud/info-12-2011/prepaid-funerals-grave-error.html

33  http://www.nbcnews.com/news/us-news/muhammad-ali-
    scripted-his-own-funeral-plans-book-n586781and
    http://www.nydailynews.com/sports/muhammad-ali-carefully-
    planned-three-day-funeral-program-article-1.2665945

34  http://peoplesmemorial.org/forms/disposition_authorization.ht
    ml

35  http://www.funeralinformationsociety.org/images/Pamplets/Wh
    at%20You%20Should%20Know%20AboutEmbalming.pdf

36  http://www.aarp.org/money/scams-fraud/info-12-
    2011/prepaid-funerals-grave-error.html

37  http://www.us-funerals.com/funeral-articles/low-cost-and-free-
    cremations.html

38  http://www.esquire.com/news-politics/news/a41147/half-of-
    americans-less-than-1000/ and
    http://www.usnews.com/news/articles/2016-07-06/the-new-
    faces-of-us-poverty

39  http://www.crainsnewyork.com/article/20160724/SMALLBIZ/
    160729946/once-seen-as-recession-proof-the-funeral-industry-is-
    in-a-death-spiral-some-owners-are-staving-off-the-end-by-
    catering-to-a-new-generations-burial-tastes

40  https://www.ssa.gov/pubs/EN-05-10008.pdf

41  http://www.benefits.va.gov/compensation/claims-special-
    burial.asp

42  http://thelawdictionary.org/article/what-happens-to-a-person-
    who-passes-away-with-no-life-insurance-money-or-family-that-
    can-help/

43  https://www.vice.com/en_us/article/its-harder-than-you-think-
    to-run-a-non-profit-funeral-home-622

44  http://www.kingcounty.gov/depts/health/examiner/indigent-
    remains.aspx

45  https://www.amazon.com/Get-Together-Organize-Records-
    Family/dp/1413323154 and https://funerals.org/product/go-
    funeral-planner-spiral-bound-includes-state-chapter-final-rights/

## CHAPTER 5: WHEN (& HOW) YOU'LL MOST LIKELY GO

1   https://www.cdc.gov/nchs/data/hus/hus15.pdf#019 and
    National Center for Health Statistics. Health, United States, 2015:

With Special Feature on Racial and Ethnic Health Disparities. Hyattsville, MD. 2016. Pg. 19

2   http://www.who.int/mediacentre/factsheets/fs310/en/index2.ht ml

3   http://www.who.int/mediacentre/factsheets/fs310/en/index2.ht ml

4   https://www.cdc.gov/nchs/fastats/leading-causes-of-death.htm

5   Sources: http://www.who.int/mediacentre/factsheets/fs310/en/ and https://www.cdc.gov/nchs/fastats/leading-causes-of-death.htm

6   The CDC and WHO use different definitions for essentially the same thing. Here's the reasoning for the difference: "CLRD actually comprises three major diseases, i.e., chronic bronchitis, emphysema, and asthma, that are all characterized by shortness of breath caused by airway obstruction. The obstruction is irreversible in chronic bronchitis and emphysema, reversible in asthma. Before 1999, CLRD was called Chronic Obstructive Pulmonary Disease (COPD). The International Classification of Diseases used by the World Health Organization (WHO) to code diseases and mortality was revised in 1999, with slight changes to the category between the 9th and 10th editions. While the two classifications are similar, COPD is used to refer to chronic bronchitis and emphysema only (for compatibility with the majority of studies cited), and CLRD is used to refer to chronic bronchitis, emphysema, and asthma." From: http://www.wvdhhr.org/bph/hsc/pubs/other/clrd/national.htm

7   The CDC defines COPD as: Chronic Obstructive Pulmonary Disease, or COPD, refers to a group of diseases that cause airflow blockage and breathing-related problems. It includes emphysema, chronic bronchitis, and in some cases asthma. Most of it is tobacco-related (cigarettes, cigars, etc.). See: https://www.cdc.gov/copd/index.html

8   https://www.cdc.gov/nchs/data/nvsr/nvsr65/nvsr65_04.pdf and https://www.cdc.gov/media/releases/2016/p1117-preventable-deaths.html

9   https://www.cdc.gov/media/releases/2016/p1117-preventable-deaths.html. See also for a compelling graphic based on older data: https://www.cdc.gov/media/releases/2014/images/p0501-preventable-deaths.pdf

10 https://www.cdc.gov/media/releases/2016/p1117-preventable-deaths.html. See also for a compelling graphic based on older data: https://www.cdc.gov/media/releases/2014/images/p0501-preventable-deaths.pdf

11 https://www.cdc.gov/injury/wisqars/fatal_help/faq.html#citation. NCHS takes about 18 months to compile, verify, and prepare the data for release to the public. After NCHS releases the data, NCIPC updates the WISQARS web pages, a process that takes a few weeks.

12 https://www.cdc.gov/injury/wisqars/leadingcauses.html. Centers for Disease Control and Prevention, National Center for Injury Prevention and Control. Web-based Injury Statistics Query and Reporting System (WISQARS) [online]. Available from URL: https://www.cdc.gov/injury/wisqars and https://www.cdc.gov/injury/wisqars/pdf/leading_causes_of_death_by_age_group_2014-a.pdf

13 https://www.cdc.gov/homeandrecreationalsafety/poisoning/

14 https://www.cdc.gov/homeandrecreationalsafety/poisoning/

15 http://www.medscape.com/viewarticle/724186

16 https://www.cdc.gov/mmwr/volumes/65/wr/mm655051e1.htm and https://www.cdc.gov/drugoverdose/pdmp/index.html

17 http://articles.latimes.com/2007/dec/22/nation/na-patch22 and http://www.pss.org.sg/whats-happening/e-bulletin/issue-no-30/drug-safety-news-fentanyl-patches

18 http://theweek.com/articles/541564/how-american-opiate-epidemic-started-by-pharmaceutical-company and http://time.com/4213760/super-bowl-opioid-commercial/ and https://www.theguardian.com/us-news/2016/oct/31/opioid-epidemic-dea-official-congress-big-pharma and http://www.wvgazettemail.com/news-health/20161217/drug-firms-poured-780m-painkillers-into-wv-amid-rise-of-overdoses and https://www.cdc.gov/mmwr/volumes/65/wr/mm655051e1.htm

19 https://www.theguardian.com/us-news/2016/oct/31/opioid-epidemic-dea-official-congress-big-pharma and http://www.asam.org/docs/default-source/advocacy/opioid-addiction-disease-facts-figures.pdf

20 https://www.cdc.gov/drugoverdose/epidemic/index.html

21  https://www.cdc.gov/media/releases/2016/p1117-preventable-deaths.html. See also for a compelling graphic based on older data: https://www.cdc.gov/media/releases/2014/images/p0501-preventable-deaths.pdf

22  https://www.cdc.gov/nchs/data/nvsr/nvsr61/nvsr61_06.pdf , see page 25, Table 5. See also: https://www.cdc.gov/nchs/data/nvsr/nvsr65/nvsr65_04.pdf , pages 44-45, Table 10.

23  https://www.cdc.gov/nchs/data/nvsr/nvsr61/nvsr61_06.pdf , see page 25, Table 5. See also: https://www.cdc.gov/nchs/data/nvsr/nvsr65/nvsr65_04.pdf , pages 44-45, Table 10.

24  Institute of Medicine (US) Committee on Palliative and End-of-Life Care for Children and Their Families; Field MJ, Behrman RE, editors. Washington (DC): National Academies Press (US); 2003. Refers to (Finkelhor and Ormrod, 2001). See: https://www.ncbi.nlm.nih.gov/books/NBK220806/

25  https://www.cdc.gov/nchs/data/dvs/lcwk9_2014.pdf and http://www.denverpost.com/2015/10/08/chart-compare-the-average-age-in-each-u-s-state-2005-2014/ .

26  http://www.denverpost.com/2015/10/08/chart-compare-the-average-age-in-each-u-s-state-2005-2014/

27  https://en.wikipedia.org/wiki/Uniform_Determination_of_Death_Act and http://www.duhaime.org/LegalDictionary/D/Death.aspx . See also: http://www.uniformlaws.org/ActSummary.aspx?title=Determination%20of%20Death%20Act

28  Gosline, Anna. "How Does It Feel to Die?" *New Scientist*, 02624079, 10/13/2007, Vol. 196, Issue 2625.

29  https://en.wikipedia.org/wiki/Reperfusion_injury and https://www.quora.com/Why-do-neurons-die-so-quickly-when-deprived-of-oxygen.

30  https://medlineplus.gov/ency/patientinstructions/000536.htm

31  http://endoflife.northwestern.edu/last_hours_of_living/part_one.pdf

32  http://endoflife.northwestern.edu/last_hours_of_living/part_one.pdf

33  Adapted from © EPEC Project,1999 Module 12: Last Hours of Living, Part 1 Page M12-7 located at

http://www.endoflife.northwestern.edu/last_hours_of_living/module12.pdf (As reprinted in: Advance planning. In: Ferris FD, Flannery JS, McNeal HB, Morissette MR, Cameron R, Bally GA, eds. Module 4: Palliative care. In: A Comprehensive Guide for the Care of Persons with HIV Disease. Toronto, Ontario: Mount Sinai Hospital and Casey House Hospice Inc; 1995:118-120. Originally published in: Freemon FR. Delirium and organic psychosis. In: Organic Mental Disease. Jamaica, NY: SP Medical and Scientific Books; 1981:81-94. )

34   http://www.endoflife.northwestern.edu/last_hours_of_living/module12.pdf

35   http://www.cancer.net/navigating-cancer-care/advanced-cancer/care-through-final-days and http://endoflife.northwestern.edu/last_hours_of_living/part_one.pdf

36   http://www.palliativecarensw.org.au/pdfs/PCNSW-Signs-Symptoms-of-Approaching-Death-ARTICLE.pdf

37   Jennie Dear. "What It Feels Like to Die: Science is just beginning to understand the experience of life's end." *The Atlantic*, SEP 9, 2016. http://www.theatlantic.com/health/archive/2016/09/what-it-feels-like-to-die/499319/?utm_source=nl-atlantic-weekly-091616

38   http://health.howstuffworks.com/diseases-conditions/death-dying/dying.htm

39   https://quizlet.com/104152558/cpr-basics-flash-cards/ and http://medical-dictionary.thefreedictionary.com/biologic+death

40   http://medical-dictionary.thefreedictionary.com/defibrillation

41   http://cpr.heart.org/AHAECC/CPRAndECC/AboutCPRFirstAid/CardiacArrestvsHeartAttack/UCM_473213_Cardiac-Arrest-vs-Heart-Attack.jsp

42   http://www.suddencardiacarrest.org/aws/SCAA/asset_manager/get_file/43858?ver=5799

43   http://health.howstuffworks.com/diseases-conditions/cardiovascular/heart/what-happens-during-a-heart-attack1.htm

44   The website of the National Cancer Institute (https://www.cancer.gov)

45   http://www.webmd.com/cancer/tc/cancer-pain-what-does-it-feel-like

46  https://www.verywell.com/dying-of-lung-cancer-what-to-expect-1132510

47  http://www.europeanlung.org/lung-disease-and-information/lung-diseases/acute-lower-respiratory-infections

48  https://www.cdc.gov/injury/images/lc-charts/leading_causes_of_death_age_group_2014_1050w760h.gif

49  http://www.bbc.co.uk/science/0/21969416

50  http://www.lung.org/lung-health-and-diseases/lung-disease-lookup/pneumonia/learn-about-pneumonia.html

51  http://www.europeanlung.org/lung-disease-and-information/lung-diseases/acute-lower-respiratory-infections

52  https://www.britannica.com/science/pneumonia

53  https://www.health.ny.gov/diseases/cardiovascular/stroke/types.htm

54  https://www.cdc.gov/stroke/types_of_stroke.htm

55  http://www.stroke.org/understand-stroke/what-stroke

56  http://www.stroke.org/understand-stroke/what-stroke

57  https://www.sharecare.com/health/stroke/is-having-stroke-painful

58  http://www.familydoctor.co.uk/unassigned-articles/stroke-complications/

59  http://www.familydoctor.co.uk/unassigned-articles/stroke-complications/

60  https://www.ncbi.nlm.nih.gov/pmc/articles/PMC3603725/

61  http://www.forensicpathologyonline.com/E-Book/asphyxia/drowning and http://emedicine.medscape.com/article/772753-overview#a3

62  http://emedicine.medscape.com/article/772753-overview#a5

63  Gosline, Anna. "How Does It Feel to Die?" *New Scientist*, 02624079, 10/13/2007, Vol. 196, Issue 2625.

64  Gosline, Anna. "How Does It Feel to Die?" *New Scientist*, 02624079, 10/13/2007, Vol. 196, Issue 2625.

65  http://www.forensicpathologyonline.com/E-Book/asphyxia/drowning and http://emedicine.medscape.com/article/772753-overview#a3

66  http://www.forensicpathologyonline.com/E-
    Book/asphyxia/drowning and
    http://emedicine.medscape.com/article/772753-overview#a3

67  http://www.encyclopedia.com/history/united-states-and-
    canada/us-government/hanging

68  http://www.medscape.com/viewarticle/774822

69  http://epmonthly.com/article/clinical-focus-strangulation-and-
    hanging-injuries/ and Vander Krol L, Wolfe R. The emergency
    department management of near-hanging victims. *J Emerg Med*
    1994;12:285-92.

70  http://www.encyclopedia.com/history/united-states-and-
    canada/us-government/hanging

71  http://www.forensicpathologyonline.com/e-
    book/asphyxia/hanging

72  http://www.forensicpathologyonline.com/e-
    book/asphyxia/hanging

73  New York-Presbyterian Hospital. Cranial Gunshot
    Wounds, http://nyp.org/health/cranial-gunshot-wounds.html.
    Testa PA, Legome E. Abdominal Trauma,
    Penetrating. http://emedicine.medscape.com/article/822099-
    overview. From
    http://www.emsworld.com/article/10319706/gunshot-wounds

74  https://www.cdc.gov/mmwr/volumes/66/wr/mm6605a2.htm
    and Gotsch KE, Annest JL, Mercy JA, Ryan GW. Surveillance for
    fatal and nonfatal firearm-related injuries—United States, 1993–
    1998. MMWR Surveill Summ 2001;50(No. SS-2).

75  http://www.emsworld.com/article/10319706/gunshot-wounds.
    See also: 8. Denton JS, Segovia A, Filkins JA. Practical pathology
    of gunshot wounds. Arch Path & Lab Med, Sep2006,
    http://findarticles.com/p/articles/mi_qa3725/is_200609/ai_n16
    717329/pg_3/. And University of Utah, Spencer S. Eccles Health
    Sciences Library. Firearms Tutorial,
    http://library.med.utah.edu/WebPath/TUTORIAL/GUNS/GU
    NINJ.html.

76  http://www.livescience.com/21774-bullet-gunshot-wound-
    survive.html

77  https://en.wikipedia.org/wiki/Ballistic_trauma and
    http://patient.info/doctor/gunshot-injuries

78 http://www.livescience.com/21774-bullet-gunshot-wound-survive.html

79 Gosline, Anna. "How Does It Feel to Die?" *New Scientist*, 02624079, 10/13/2007, Vol. 196, Issue 2625.

80 Gosline, Anna. "How Does It Feel to Die?" *New Scientist*, 02624079, 10/13/2007, Vol. 196, Issue 2625.

81 http://science.howstuffworks.com/cremation1.htm

82 http://www.forensicpathologyonline.com/E-Book/injuries/thermal-injuries

83 http://www.cbsnews.com/news/gas-explosions-not-uncommon/

84 http://www.forensicpathologyonline.com/E-Book/injuries/bombblast-inuries

85 http://emedicine.medscape.com/article/822587-overview

86 http://patient.info/doctor/blast-injury#ref-2

87 https://www.cdc.gov/masstrauma/preparedness/primer.pdf

88 https://www.acep.org/blastinjury/

89 https://en.wikipedia.org/wiki/Penetrating_trauma

90 http://www.forensicmed.co.uk/wounds/sharp-force-trauma/stab-wounds/

91 http://www.forensicmed.co.uk/wounds/sharp-force-trauma/stab-wounds/

92 http://www.forensicmed.co.uk/wounds/sharp-force-trauma/stab-wounds/

93 http://woundcaresociety.org/how-likely-are-you-to-survive-a-stab-wound

94 http://www.forensicmed.co.uk/wounds/sharp-force-trauma/stab-wounds/

95 http://www.forensicmed.co.uk/wounds/sharp-force-trauma/stab-wounds/

96 https://www.ncbi.nlm.nih.gov/pubmed/3744212?dopt=AbstractPlus

97 http://www.forensicmed.co.uk/wounds/sharp-force-trauma/stab-wounds/

98 https://www.cdc.gov/motorvehiclesafety/impaired_driving/impaired-drv_factsheet.html Based on 2014 data. See also:

https://crashstats.nhtsa.dot.gov/Api/Public/ViewPublication/81 2231

99  https://www.bostonglobe.com/metro/2016/03/08/pedestrian-fatalities-rising-faster-than-ever-before-study-says/AjfBkW7WPhKsvvbwweL7UP/story.html

100  https://www.cdc.gov/mmwr/preview/mmwrhtml/mm6431a1.ht m and Beck LF, Dellinger AM, O'Neil ME. Motor vehicle crash injury rates by mode of travel, United States: using exposure-based methods to quantify differences. *Am J Epidemiol* 2007;166:212–8.

101  http://www.iihs.org/iihs/topics/t/pedestrians-and-bicyclists/fatalityfacts/bicycles

102  http://emedicine.medscape.com/article/1765532-overview#a5

103  http://emedicine.medscape.com/article/1765532-overview#a5

104  http://emedicine.medscape.com/article/1765532-overview#a5

105  http://emedicine.medscape.com/article/1765532-overview#a5

106  http://emedicine.medscape.com/article/1765532-overview#a5

107  http://www.exploreforensics.co.uk/electrocution.html

108  Gosline, Anna. "How Does It Feel to Die?" *New Scientist*, 02624079, 10/13/2007, Vol. 196, Issue 2625.

109  http://misc.medscape.com/pi/iphone/medscapeapp/html/A770 179-business.html and https://thehealthscience.com/topics/electrical-injuries-emergency-medicine

110  http://emedicine.medscape.com/article/770179-overview#a5

111  http://emedicine.medscape.com/article/1975728-overview

112  http://www.lightningsafety.noaa.gov/struck.shtml

113  http://emedicine.medscape.com/article/1975728-overview

114  http://www.lightningsafety.noaa.gov/ and http://www.lightningsafety.noaa.gov/struck.shtml and http://www.lightningsafety.noaa.gov/fatalities/analysis06-15.pdf

115  http://www.healthguidance.org/entry/17291/1/What-Happens-to-Your-Body-When-You-Get-Electrocuted.html

116  http://emedicine.medscape.com/article/770179-overview#a2

117  http://medind.nic.in/jal/t13/i1/jalt13i1p47.pdf

118  https://www.facs.org/quality%20programs/trauma/ipc/falls

119 https://msrc.fsu.edu/system/files/Turk%20et%20al %202004%20Pathological%20features%20of%20fatal%20falls %20from%20height.pdf

120 Turner, P. "A fall from a cliff three hundred and twenty feet high without fatal injuries." *Guy's Hosp Gaz* 1919;33:27–80.

121 Rich, Jeremy, Dorothy E. Dean, and Robert H. Powers. Forensic Medicine of the Lower Extremity: Human Identification and Trauma Analysis of the Thigh, Leg, and Foot. Totowa, N.J.: Humana Press, 2005. <http://public.eblib.com/choice/publicfullrecord.aspx? p=603277>.

122 https://msrc.fsu.edu/system/files/Turk%20et%20al %202004%20Pathological%20features%20of%20fatal%20falls %20from%20height.pdf

123 Gosline, Anna. "How Does It Feel to Die?" *New Scientist*, 02624079, 10/13/2007, Vol. 196, Issue 2625.

124 http://injuryprevention.bmj.com/content/6/1/62.3.long

125 https://msrc.fsu.edu/system/files/Turk%20et%20al %202004%20Pathological%20features%20of%20fatal%20falls %20from%20height.pdf

126 https://msrc.fsu.edu/system/files/Turk%20et%20al %202004%20Pathological%20features%20of%20fatal%20falls %20from%20height.pdf

127 http://emedicine.medscape.com/article/166464-overview#a5

128 https://www.cdc.gov/nchs/data/databriefs/db273.pdf

129 http://www.webmd.com/mental-health/addiction/drug-overdose-naloxone#1

130 https://www.ncbi.nlm.nih.gov/pmc/articles/PMC3739053/

131 http://www.webmd.com/mental-health/addiction/drug-overdose-naloxone#1

132 http://emedicine.medscape.com/article/815784-overview#a7

133 http://www.livestrong.com/article/234224-the-effects-of-a-sleeping-pill-overdose/

134 http://science.howstuffworks.com/autopsy3.htm and http://www.npr.org/2011/02/02/133403760/coroners-dont-need-degrees-to-determine-death and http://www.npr.org/2011/02/03/131242432/graphics-how-is-death-investigated-in-your-state

135 http://science.howstuffworks.com/autopsy3.htm and
http://www.npr.org/2011/02/02/133403760/coroners-dont-
need-degrees-to-determine-death and
http://www.npr.org/2011/02/03/131242432/graphics-how-is-
death-investigated-in-your-state

## CHAPTER 6 – YOU'RE DEAD. NOW WHAT?

1   http://www.genesisstory.com/Basic_Biology_Concepts/Death_a
nd_Dying/Physiology.htm

2   http://aboutforensics.co.uk/decomposition/ and
http://laphamsquarterly.org/death/maps/departures and
https://en.wikipedia.org/wiki/Decomposition and
http://www.exploreforensics.co.uk/the-rate-of-decay-in-a-
corpse.html

3   https://en.wikipedia.org/wiki/Decomposition

4   Santarsiero, A., Minelli, L., Cutilli, D. and Cappielo, G. "Hygienic
aspects related to burial." Microchem. J. 67, 2000. and Micozzi,
M.S.. Postmortem Change in Human and Animal Remains: A
Systematic Approach. Springfield, IL: Charles C. Thomas, 1991.

5   http://aboutforensics.co.uk/decomposition/

6   http://aboutforensics.co.uk/decomposition/

7   http://www.forensicpathologyonline.com/e-book/post-mortem-
changes/putrefaction

8   http://www.forensicpathologyonline.com/e-book/post-mortem-
changes/putrefaction

## CHAPTER 7 – NEXT STEPS FOR SURVIVORS

1   http://www.organtransplants.org/understanding/death/

2   http://www.endoflife.northwestern.edu/last_hours_of_living/part_t
wo.cfm

3   https://www.funeral-burial-insurance.com/Funeral-Planning-
Checklist.pdf

4   http://www.endoflife.northwestern.edu/last_hours_of_living/pa
rt_two.cfm

5   http://diesmart.com/sayinggoodbye/immediately-after-death/#registration

6   http://diesmart.com/sayinggoodbye/immediately-after-death/

7   http://diesmart.com/sayinggoodbye/immediately-after-death/#registration

8   https://www.epa.gov/ocean-dumping/burial-sea and https://www.epa.gov/ocean-dumping/burial-sea#instructions.

9   http://science.howstuffworks.com/cremation1.htm

10  http://www.summum.org/cost.shtml and http://www.dailymail.co.uk/ news/article-2110566/Modern-day-mummies-The-craze-attracting-celebrities-pet-owners-keen-preserving-bodies.html

11  http://abcnews.go.com/US/story?id=91481&page=1 and http://science.howstuffworks.com/life/genetic/cryonics2.htm

12  http://www.promessa.se/news/ and https://en.wikipedia.org/wiki/Promession

13  http://www.nolo.com/legal-encyclopedia/how-get-death-certificate.html

14  http://diesmart.com/sayinggoodbye/immediately-after-death/#registration

15  http://www.legalvoice.org/after-death-occurs-checklist

16  http://www.dow.com/friends/pdfs/Funeral_Planning_Guide.pdf

17  http://www.dow.com/friends/pdfs/Funeral_Planning_Guide.pdf

## CHAPTER 8 – THE SCIENCE OF LOSS

1   http://www.calebwilde.com/2013/10/ten-things-about-embalming/

2   The Week. "Flight 370: First Piece in the Puzzle?" 8/15/2015.

3   http://www.endoflife.northwestern.edu/last_hours_of_living/part_three.cfm

4   http://content.time.com/time/magazine/article/0,9171,2042372,00.html and http://www.apa.org/helpcenter/grief.aspx

5   http://content.time.com/time/magazine/article/0,9171,2042372,00.html and http://www.apa.org/helpcenter/grief.aspx

6    http://content.time.com/time/magazine/article/0,9171,2042372
,00.html and http://www.apa.org/helpcenter/grief.aspx

7    http://content.time.com/time/magazine/article/0,9171,2042372
,00.html and http://www.apa.org/helpcenter/grief.aspx

8    http://content.time.com/time/magazine/article/0,9171,2042372
-4,00.html. This article originally appeared in the Jan. 24, 2011
issue of TIME. Adapted from *The Truth About Grief*, by Ruth
Davis Konigsberg. © 2011. Published by Simon & Schuster Inc.

## CHAPTER 9 – NOTHING LASTS FOREVER

1    https://www.theguardian.com/lifeandstyle/2015/mar/01/what-
does-it-feel-like-to-die

2    http://endoflife.northwestern.edu/last_hours_of_living/part_on
e.pdf

3    Phil Plait. "Don't Be a Dick." From TAM 8, Oct. 8-11, 2010.
https://www.youtube.com/watch?v=FrFRbGjUtJk. The
comment is at the 5:32 minute mark.

4    Framingham, Julie, and Martell L. Teasley. *Behavioral Health
Response to Disasters*. Boca Raton: CRC Press, 2012. Section 6.5.2.2
Identification with Large Collectives and Their Cultural Value
Systems

5    Burton, Robert Alan. *On Being Certain: Believing You Are Right Even
When You're Not*. New York: St. Martin's Press, 2008. Pg. 106.

# BIBLIOGRAPHY

Aristotle, John Baxter, and George Whalley. *Aristotle's Poetics*. Montréal: McGill-Queen's University Press, 2014.

Burton, Robert Alan. *On Being Certain: Believing You Are Right Even When You're Not*. New York: St. Martin's Griffin, 2009.

Cullen, Melanie, and Shae Irving. *Get It Together: Organize Your Records So Your Family Won't Have To*. 2005.

Framingham, Julie, and Martell L. Teasley. *Behavioral Health Response to Disasters*. Hoboken: Taylor and Francis, 2013.

Funeral Consumers Alliance. *Before I Go, You Should Know*. 2013.

Konigsberg, Ruth Davis. *The Truth About Grief: The Myth of Its Five Stages and the New Science of Loss*. New York: Simon & Schuster, 2014.

Rich, Jeremy. *Forensic Medicine of the Lower Extremity: Human Identification and Trauma Analysis of the Thigh, Leg, and Foot*. Totowa, NJ: Humana Press, 2013.

Shelley, Percy Bysshe, and Neville Rogers. *The Complete Poetical Works of Percy Bysshe Shelley: In Four Volumes*. Oxford: Clarendon Press, 1972.

# INDEX

## A

# B

# C

# D

# E

# F

# G

# H

www.ingramcontent.com/pod-product-compliance
Lightning Source LLC
Chambersburg PA
CBHW030435290526
45786CB00001B/298

* 9 7 8 1 5 4 2 8 7 9 6 7 5 *